Luke ▭▭▭▭ ▭ ▭ ▭▭▭▭▭, ▭▭▭▭▭ ▭▭▭ ▭▭▭▭▭▭▭ ▭
internationally known for both productions of Shakespeare
and site-specific work. He has directed and led workshops on
Shakespeare around the world, from *A Midsummer Night's
Dream* in Brazil to *Macbeth* in Hong Kong via *Pericles* in
South Africa.

Luke is Artistic Director of Theatre Nomad and a regular
actor at London's Actors Centre. He is author of *Play-
Acting: A Guide to Theatre Workshops*. For more information,
see www.lukedixon.co.uk

## THE GOOD AUDITION GUIDES

CLASSICAL MONOLOGUES
edited by Marina Caldarone

SHAKESPEARE MONOLOGUES
edited by Luke Dixon

MODERN MONOLOGUES
edited by Jane Maud

The Good Audition Guides

# SHAKESPEARE MONOLOGUES FOR MEN

*edited and introduced by*

LUKE DIXON

## NICK HERN BOOKS

London

www.nickhernbooks.co.uk

A NICK HERN BOOK

*The Good Audition Guides:*
*Shakespeare Monologues for Men*
first published in Great Britain in 2009
by Nick Hern Books Limited
14 Larden Road, London W3 7ST

Introduction copyright © 2009 Luke Dixon
Copyright in this selection © 2009 Nick Hern Books Ltd

Cover design: www.energydesignstudio.com

Typeset by Country Setting, Kingsdown, Kent, CT14 8ES
Printed and bound in Great Britain by CPI Bookmarque,
Croydon, Surrey

A CIP catalogue record for this book
is available from the British Library

ISBN 978 1 84842 005 2

# Contents

6

THE TRAGEDIES

# Introduction

## WHY SHAKESPEARE? ☞

The basic requirements for most auditions, from drama-school entry to a season at the recreated Globe Theatre in London, will include performing a speech by Shakespeare. Faced with the thirty-eight plays that are generally considered to have been written by Shakespeare, it is daunting for even the most experienced actor to know where to begin finding a suitable speech. Thirty-six of those plays were collected after Shakespeare's death by his colleagues and printed in what is known as the First Folio, a folio being the size of the sheet of paper it was printed on. Around 750 copies were produced and they sold for £1 each. About 230 still exist and now sell for around £3 million each. A couple of other plays only appeared in what are known as quarto editions, on paper folded to half the size of a folio sheet.

The Shakespearean canon, all the plays he wrote which have survived, is the heart of English drama. A speech from one of those plays can provide an actor with opportunities to show off their skills and talent in a whole range of ways: vocally and physically, in terms of characterisation and storytelling, emotionally and intellectually. A speech by Shakespeare is the best tool for an actor to demonstrate their craft, and for an audition panel or director to appreciate and judge it.

## CHOOSING YOUR MONOLOGUE ☞

In this volume I have brought together fifty speeches, from amongst the best known to the least common. You will never find a 'new' Shakespeare speech. For one thing, fashion and contemporary performance are often factors that make speeches currently popular; for another, never second-guess what speech the actor before or after you will perform. Best to find a speech that you like, enjoy performing and can in some way empathise with. Do not worry about what other actors are doing.

Choose more than one speech (maybe one comedy, one history and one tragedy) to have in your repertoire so that you always have something suitable when the call comes. Having chosen a speech, you *must* read the play and find the backstory so you know where the character and the speech are coming from.

*Complexity*    Some of the speeches in this book are relatively simple and might be more useful for the actor for whom Shakespeare is a new and terrifying experience: Proteus in *The Two Gentlemen of Verona* and Bottom in *A Midsummer Night's Dream* perhaps fall into this category. Others, like Hamlet and Othello, are rich and complex in their language, thought and emotion and might be more suitable for actors seeking a challenge or needing to show the full range of their abilities.

*Age*    It is rare that we know the age of a character in a play by Shakespeare. Juliet we are told is fourteen. Otherwise ages are for the most part relative. Hamlet is younger than his uncle Claudius who has murdered his father. Proteus and Valentine in *The Two Gentlemen of Verona*, friends in love with the same girl, are of an age. Caliban, the monster in *The Tempest*, could be any age. In a production the director will have made decisions about the age of his characters and their relative ages to each other, and may ask you to approximate a particular age. In an audition you can be much more flexible in deciding whether the speech of a character is suited to you and your playing age. To give you some guidance I have listed below 'younger' and 'older' characters whose speeches are in this book. I have done the same with status ('higher' and 'lower'). I have also identified the speeches with the most obvious comic potential.

*Length*    The speeches vary considerably in the number of their words but not necessarily in the time they take to perform. Falstaff's speech in *The Merry Wives of Windsor* as he enters the inn dripping wet from a soaking in the Thames, though short of words contains a great deal of implied action, and the action becomes as important as the words when you are performing it. It is a speech that needs to be given space to breathe and for the spaces and silences within it to be found. In this and many other speeches there are important moments when the character is listening (Oberon in *A Midsummer Night's Dream* as he waits for Puck to bring him the flower) or when he is waiting for or expecting a reply (Prince Escalus in *Romeo and Juliet* and Angelo in *Measure for Measure*). These moments can make a speech come fully alive.

Where some speeches are too long for audition purposes I have, as judiciously as possible, made cuts.

LANGUAGE ☞

Shakespeare's audiences went to 'hear' plays. It was not until long after his death that anyone wrote of going to 'see' a play. So the sounds of Shakespeare's words are as important as their meanings. Indeed the sounds often help convey the meanings. Enjoy and play with the sounds as you work through the speeches.

*Prose* is everyday speech but Shakespeare often heightens that speech, giving it colour, richness, images and so on that we would not use in our everyday lives. Some of the speeches in this book are entirely in prose including Trinculo in *The Tempest*, Benedick in *Much Ado About Nothing* and the Boy in *Henry V*.

*Poetry* is where that heightened use of language is taken further and the speech goes beyond the everyday, and rhythm and rhyme become important.

*Verse* is poetry where the rhythms of the words are organised.

*Iambic pentameter* is a particular kind of verse. An 'iamb' is where a short syllable is followed by a long syllable giving a 'di–dum' rhythm. 'Metre' is how rhythms are organised in lines of verse. 'Penta' is the old Greek word for five. So if you put five iambs in a line of verse you get an iambic pentameter:

*di-dum, di-dum, di-dum, di-dum, di-dum*

This was the main form Shakespeare used in writing his plays: they are the heartbeat of his language. Sometimes it is used rigidly and is easy to spot:

> Your grace shall pardon me, I will not back.
> I am too high-born to be propertied
>
> (Lewis the Dauphin, *King John*)

Sometimes, especially as he got older and more experienced, Shakespeare played with the form and pulled it around for emotional, dramatic or characterisation effect.

In order for the rhythm to work, a word ending in '–ed' will sometimes have the letters stressed as a syllable, in which case it is printed '–èd', and sometimes it will not be a separate syllable but be spoken as if the 'e' is not there, in which case it is printed '–'d'

*Rhyming couplets*   Sometimes Shakespeare uses rhyme and when two lines rhyme together, we have a rhyming couplet. Often these are used at the end of a speech or scene to indicate finality.

*Punctuation* in Shakespeare is a controversial subject. Shakespeare did not prepare his plays for publication and therefore the punctuation in the texts is largely put there by his colleagues or the publisher or printer. Nonetheless, the punctuation in the speeches I have chosen, which follow for the most part the First Folio, can give you some help not just with sense but also with where to breathe, pause, rest, change gear or change thought.

*Vocabulary*   Shakespeare wrote at a time when English as we know it was developing rapidly. He made up or used for the first time many words and phrases that have become part of our everyday speech. Words that were brand new when Shakespeare used them include: accommodation, critic, dwindle, eventful, exposure, frugal, generous, gloomy, laughable, majestic, misplaced, monumental, multitudinous and obscene. Phrases that he coined include: disgraceful conduct, elbow-room, fair play, green-eyed monster, method in his madness, to thine own self be true, the lady doth protest too much, and it's Greek to me. Some of the words he used or invented have faded from the language, and some words which are familiar today had different or stronger meanings then than now. In both these cases, I have glossed their meanings in the notes.

THE AUDITION ☞

*Thought process*    It is rare that a character sets out to make a speech, though in some of the big public and political scenes a character does just that. Henry V has to make a speech in front of his court when he opens the gift of tennis balls from the French king, and Prince Escalus has come prepared to read the riot act to the warring Capulets and Montagues. But for the most part a speech starts with a single thought which is followed by another and then another until the character has said enough – or been interrupted. Allow time for each of those thoughts to come and be fresh in the mind before they are spoken. Do not be daunted by what can seem endless lines of text. It is not a race to get through to the end. Take the speech one thought at a time.

*Structure*    As you follow the thoughts, follow too the emotions and language of the speech. Look for its structure. Allow yourself to show the full range of emotion and vocal possibility within the speech. Seek variety. None of these speeches is on one note. All allow a wide range of vocal and emotional expression.

*Setting and geography*    Many of these speeches are soliloquies allowing the character to express his thoughts or ideas to an audience while he is alone, such as Edmund in *King Lear*. Other speeches, like Angelo's in *Measure for Measure*, are parts of dialogues or conversations. And some, such as Richmond's in *Richard III*, are directed to large public gatherings. Others may be a combination of all these. Decide who else, if anyone, is there to hear the speech and where they are placed. Give thought to the geography or layout of the place the speech is being spoken in – whether the woods of *A Midsummer Night's Dream*, the court of King Henry IV, or the windswept island of *The Tempest*. Take a few moments when you first come into the audition room to place the other characters and recreate the geography and setting in your mind's eye (another phrase Shakespeare coined).

*Audience*    If your speech is directed to an audience, it can be a theatre audience or an audience within the scene. Some speeches are soliloquies which can be played to oneself, to the audience or some combination of the two (Sebastian in *Twelfth Night*). Others, such as Petruchio in *The Taming of the Shrew* and Launce in *The Two Gentlemen of Verona*, are clearly to an audience in the theatre. Others are to a public audience within the play, like the King in *Richard II* and Mark Antony in *Julius Caesar*. Decide whether and how to use your audition panel as that audience.

*Make the space your own*    Many other actors will have been in the audition room before you. Many will come after you. Spend a moment or two before you start your speech by focusing and allowing the panel to focus on you. Create the silence out of which your words will come and decide on the energy that the words will bring with them, whether the quiet of the night as King Henry IV tries to sleep or the storm that is engulfing Trinculo on the beach in *The Tempest*.

HOW TO USE THIS BOOK

For each speech I have given an indication of:

WHERE ☞    If possible I have indicated where and when the action is taking place. Sometimes this can be very specific, either because Shakespeare has told us or because the action is tied to a particular historical event. If the plays are set in times of legend, the date and place are of no direct importance in affecting how you perform them.

WHO ELSE IS THERE ☞    This note gives an indication of who else is on stage and the character's relationship to them.

WHAT IS HAPPENING ☞    This note will give a context for the speech but it is not a substitute for reading the play and yourself deciding where the speech is coming from.

WHAT TO THINK ABOUT ☞    I have indicated some ideas of things to think about as you are working on the speech. This is by no means an exhaustive list but will give you a way into the speech and should spark other thoughts and ideas of your own.

WHERE ELSE TO LOOK ☞    If you like a speech or character and want to look elsewhere in this collection for similar pieces, this will help you on your way.

GLOSSARY ☞    I have glossed the trickier and more perplexing words, phrases and thoughts in the speeches, but do not worry if you need a dictionary or annotated edition of the play to help you fully understand what your character is saying.

THE TEXTS ☞    Wherever possible I have used the exemplary texts of *The Shakespeare Folios* published by Nick Hern Books and edited by Nick de Somogyi, and the speeches appear in the order that they do in the First Folio (comedies, then histories, then tragedies). Speeches from plays not yet published in this series have been edited by me from the First Folio using the same editorial rules. In the case of *Pericles*, which does not appear in the First Folio and which is of contested authorship, I have used the Quarto text edited in the same way. All the glosses are my own.

The following categories may help you when looking for a particular attribute that suits you or the purposes of your monologue:

- OLDER

  Falstaff in *The Merry Wives of Windsor*
  Leonato in *Much Ado About Nothing*
  Shepherd in *The Winter's Tale*
  Pericles in *Pericles*
  King Henry in *King Henry IV, Part Two*
  Wolsey in *Henry VIII*
  Claudius in *Hamlet*

- YOUNGER

  Proteus in *The Two Gentlemen of Verona*
  Valentine in *The Two Gentlemen of Verona*
  Sebastian in *Twelfth Night*
  Hotspur in *King Henry IV, Part One*
  Boy in *Henry V*
  Troilus in *Troilus and Cressida*
  Hamlet in *Hamlet*

- HIGHER STATUS

  Angelo in *Measure for Measure*
  Oberon in *A Midsummer Night's Dream*
  King Richard in *Richard II*
  Prince Escalus in *Romeo and Juliet*

- LOWER STATUS

  Launce in *The Two Gentlemen of Verona*
  Bottom in *A Midsummer Night's Dream*
  Boy in *Henry V*

- COMIC

  Launce in *The Two Gentlemen of Verona*
  Falstaff in *The Merry Wives of Windsor*
  Benedick in *Much Ado About Nothing*
  Don Armado in *Love's Labour's Lost*
  Berowne in *Love's Labour's Lost*
  Bottom in *A Midsummer Night's Dream*
  Jaques in *As You Like It*
  Petruchio in *The Taming of the Shrew*
  Shepherd in *The Winter's Tale*

# The Comedies

# The Tempest

WHO ☞    *Caliban, a savage and deformed slave.*

WHERE ☞    *Somewhere on Prospero's island.*

WHO ELSE IS THERE ☞    *Caliban is alone.*

WHAT IS HAPPENING ☞    *Caliban curses Prospero who has taken his island home from him and made him a prisoner. He is persecuted by Prospero's servant spirits who take different forms (such as apes and hedgehogs) to cause him pain.*

WHAT TO THINK ABOUT ☞

- *The bogs, fens and flats are real places on the island that is Caliban's home.*

- *Decide how he uses his senses and so how he is aware that something is coming to torment him. This could be through sight, smell or sound and may be quite animal-like.*

- *Caliban's torment is both a physical and a mental one.*

- *Think about how much pain Caliban may be in and how this will affect his movement.*

- *Explore Caliban's physicality; what he looks like, moves like and sounds like.*

WHERE ELSE TO LOOK ☞    *Another speech filled with the pain of torment is Titus (Titus Andronicus, p. 90).*

## *Caliban*

**❝** All the infections that the sun sucks up
From bogs, fens, flats, on Prosper fall, and make him
By inch-meal* a disease! His spirits hear me,
And yet I needs must curse. But they'll nor pinch,
Fright me with urchin-shows,* pitch me i'th' mire,
Nor lead me, like a firebrand, in the dark
Out of my way, unless he bid 'em; but
For every trifle are they set upon me,
Sometime like apes, that mow* and chatter at me,
And after bite me. Then like hedgehogs, which
Lie tumbling in my barefoot way, and mount
Their pricks at my footfall. Sometime am I
All wound with adders, who with cloven tongues
Do hiss me into madness. Lo, now, lo,
Here comes a spirit of his, and to torment me
For bringing wood in slowly. I'll lie flat –
Perchance he will not mind me. **❞**

*(Act 2, scene 2, lines 1–17)*

GLOSSARY

*inch-meal* – inch by inch
*urchin-shows* – apparitions
*mow* – make faces

# The Tempest

WHO ☞  *Trinculo, a jester. Part of a group shipwrecked on a remote island.*

WHERE ☞  *The sea-shore of Prospero's island.*

WHO ELSE IS THERE ☞  *Caliban, a savage and deformed slave, hiding under a blanket.*

WHAT IS HAPPENING ☞  *Seeking shelter from the coming storm, the jester Trinculo finds what he thinks at first to be a fish and then an islander hiding under a cloak or blanket. It is in fact the 'monster' Caliban. As thunder strikes, Trinculo decides to hide under the blanket himself.*

WHAT TO THINK ABOUT ☞

- *There are great opportunities for physical comedy with this speech.*
- *Create a sense of there being a great storm.*
- *Trinculo is caught between the storm and possible shelter.*
- *Trinculo does not know what is under the cloak.*
- *Touching the cloth and what is underneath it may take great courage.*
- *Much can be made of the fish-like smell that comes from under the blanket.*
- *Decide whether Trinculo is talking to himself or to the audience as well.*

WHERE ELSE TO LOOK ☞  *Edgar (King Lear, p. 112) also seeks shelter from a storm.*

## Trinculo

**❝** Here's neither bush nor shrub to bear off any weather at all. And another storm brewing, I hear it sing i'th' wind. Yond same black cloud, yond huge one, looks like a foul bombard* that would shed his liquor. If it should thunder as it did before, I know not where to hide my head. Yond same cloud cannot choose but fall by pailfuls. What have we here, a man, or a fish? Dead or alive? A fish, he smells like a fish. A very ancient and fish-like smell. A kind of not-of-the-newest Poor-John.* A strange fish. Were I in England now, as once I was, and had but this fish painted,* not a holiday fool there but would give a piece of silver. There would this monster, make a man. Any strange beast there makes a man. When they will not give a doit* to relieve a lame beggar, they will lay out ten to see a dead Indian.* Legged like a man, and his fins like arms! Warm, o' my troth! I do now let loose my opinion, hold it no longer: this is no fish, but an islander, that hath lately suffered by a thunderbolt.

*Thunder.*

Alas, the storm is come again! My best way is to creep under his gaberdine.* There is no other shelter hereabout. Misery acquaints a man with strange bed-fellows. I will here shroud till the dregs of the storm be past. **❞**

(*Act 2, scene 2, line 18 onwards*)

GLOSSARY

*bombard* – big leather bag containing wine
*Poor-John* – dried fish
*fish painted* – a painting of the fish
*doit* – coin of very little value
*they will lay out ten to see a dead Indian* – people will pay ten times the
    amount they will refuse to give to a beggar to see a curiosity
*gaberdine* – cloak

# The Two Gentlemen of Verona

WHO ☞ *Proteus, a young gentlemen of Verona.*

WHERE ☞ *The Duke's Palace in Milan.*

WHO ELSE IS THERE ☞ *Proteus is alone.*

WHAT IS HAPPENING ☞ *Though in love with Julia, Proteus has just seen Silvia, the new girlfriend of his best friend Valentine, and has immediately fallen for her.*

WHAT TO THINK ABOUT ☞

- *A moment ago, Proteus was in love with Julia.*

- *He could be surprised by his sudden change of affections or this may be something that happens to him regularly.*

- *Decide how strong his friendship with Valentine is and how much he is prepared to risk that friendship.*

- *What does Silvia looks like? Paint a picture for yourself of the things that Proteus finds so attractive about her.*

- *There is a break after 'she is fair'. Use it to think about Silvia before the thought of Julia comes into Proteus's mind.*

- *Decide how much Proteus wants to fight his feelings and how much he is ready to indulge them.*

- *Play with the word 'compass' which has a multitude of meanings – to encircle, to find the whereabouts of, to understand, to achieve something; and it is an instrument with a sharp point.*

WHERE ELSE TO LOOK ☞ *Other lovers include Proteus's friend Valentine (The Two Gentlemen of Verona, p. 26) in love with the same woman, and Troilus (Troilus and Cressida, p. 88).*

## *Proteus*

**"** Even as one heat another heat expels,
Or as one nail by strength drives out another,
So the remembrance of my former love
Is by a newer object quite forgotten.
Is it mine eye, or Valentine's praise,
Her true perfection, or my false transgression,
That makes me reasonless, to reason thus?
She is fair. And so is Julia that I love,
That I did love, for now my love is thaw'd,
Which like a waxen image 'gainst a fire
Bears no impression of the thing it was.
Methinks my zeal to Valentine is cold,
And that I love him not as I was wont.
O, but I love his lady too, too much,
And that's the reason I love him so little.
How shall I dote on* her with more advice,*
That thus without advice begin to love her?
'Tis but her picture* I have yet beheld,
And that hath dazzled my reason's light.
But when I look on her perfections,
There is no reason but I shall be blind.
If I can check my erring love, I will;
If not, to compass her I'll use my skill. **"**

*(Act 2, scene 4, lines 191–213)*

GLOSSARY

*dote on* – be infatuated with
*advice* – thought, reflection
*picture* – appearance

# The Two Gentlemen of Verona

WHO ☞ *Launce, a clownish servant to Proteus, a young gentleman of Verona.*

WHERE ☞ *A street in Verona.*

WHO ELSE IS THERE ☞ *Crab, his dog.*

WHAT IS HAPPENING ☞ *Alone on stage with his dog Crab, Launce tells the audience of his pet's misdeeds.*

WHAT TO THINK ABOUT ☞

- *Launce is talking to the audience about his dog. The speech would have been written for one of the regular clowns in Shakespeare's company and might well have been partly improvised.*

- *Think about why his dog is so important to him and why he is prepared to make the sacrifices for it that he does.*

- *Characterise all the other people in the story through their voices and their physicality.*

- *The speech finishes quite intimately with Launce talking directly to Crab, perhaps forgetting the audience.*

WHERE ELSE TO LOOK ☞ *Trinculo's speech (The Tempest, p. 20) is another comic conversation with the audience.*

### Launce

**❝** When a man's servant shall play the cur* with him, look you, it goes hard. One that I brought up of a puppy. One that I saved from drowning, when three or four of his blind brothers and sisters went to it. I have taught him, even as one would say precisely, 'Thus I would teach a dog.' I was sent to deliver him, as a present to Mistress Silvia from my master, and I came no sooner into the dining-chamber but he steps me to her trencher* and steals her capon's leg.* O, 'tis a foul thing, when a cur cannot keep himself in all companies! I would have, as one should say, one that takes upon him to be a dog indeed, to be, as it were, a dog at all things. If I had not had more wit than he, to take a fault upon me that he did, I think verily he had been hanged for't. Sure as I live, he had suffered for't. You shall judge.

He thrusts me himself into the company of three or four gentlemanlike dogs under the Duke's table. He had not been there, bless the mark*, a pissing while, but all the chamber smelt him. 'Out with the dog!' says one. 'What cur is that?' says another. 'Whip him out,' says the third. 'Hang him up,' says the Duke. I, having been acquainted with the smell before, knew it was Crab, and goes me to the fellow that whips the dogs. 'Friend,' quoth I, 'you mean to whip the dog?' 'Ay, marry, do I,' quoth he. 'You do him the more wrong,' quoth I; ''twas I did the thing you wot* of.' He makes me no more ado, but whips me out of the chamber. How many masters would do this for his servant? Nay, I'll be sworn, I have sat in the stocks for puddings he hath stolen, otherwise he had been executed. I have stood on the pillory for geese he hath killed, otherwise he had suffered for't.

(*To Crab*) Thou thinkest not of this now. Nay, I remember the trick you served me when I took my leave of Madam Silvia. Did not I bid thee still mark me, and do as I do? When didst thou see me heave up my leg, and make water against a gentlewoman's farthingale? Didst thou ever see me do such a trick? 🔊

(*Act 4, scene 4, line 1 onwards*)

GLOSSARY

*cur* – dog (Launce is saying that it's hard when the master and the dog have their roles reversed)
*steps me to her trencher* – steps over me to get to her plate
*capon* – roast chicken
*bless the mark* – excuse my language (polite phrase)
*wot* – know

# The Two Gentlemen of Verona

WHO ☞ *Valentine, a young gentleman of Verona.*

WHERE ☞ *Somewhere in the forest outside Verona.*

WHO ELSE IS THERE ☞ *Valentine is alone.*

WHAT ELSE IS HAPPENING ☞ *Escaping into the forest to avoid the anger of the Duke, his girlfriend's father, Valentine thinks of the girl he has left behind.*

WHAT TO THINK ABOUT ☞

- *Valentine is completely absorbed in his love of Silvia, whom he addresses directly ('thou').*

- *Picture what Silvia looks like and what the qualities are that make him love her so much.*

- *Work out the geography of where Valentine is (how far from town and everybody else) and the detail of the forest around him.*

- *When he asks 'what halloing?' it is because he thinks he hears the outlaws he has befriended in the forest chasing a traveller.*

- *Decide whether he can shout of his love without being heard and whether he is comfortable in so wild a place.*

WHERE ELSE TO LOOK ☞ *His friend Proteus (The Two Gentlemen of Verona, p. 22) is in love with the same woman. Troilus (Troilus and Cressida, p. 88) is also overwhelmed by love.*

## *Valentine*

**66** How use doth breed a habit in a man!
This shadowy desert, unfrequented woods,
I better brook* than flourishing peopled towns.
Here can I sit alone, unseen of any,
And to the nightingale's complaining notes
Tune my distresses, and record my woes.
O thou that dost inhabit in my breast,
Leave not the mansion so long tenantless,
Lest, growing ruinous, the building fall,
And leave no memory of what it was.
Repair me, with thy presence, Silvia.
Thou gentle nymph, cherish thy forlorn swain!*
What halloing,* and what stir is this today?
These are my mates, that make their wills their law,*
Have some unhappy passenger in chase.
They love me well. Yet I have much to do
To keep them from uncivil outrages.*
Withdraw thee, Valentine. Who's this comes here? **99**

*(Act 5, scene 4, lines 1–18)*

GLOSSARY

*brook* – tolerate
*swain* – lover
*halloing* – shouting
*that make their wills their law* – who live as outlaws
*uncivil outrages* – criminal violence (Valentine is saying he has a lot of
   work to do to reform these outlaws)

# The Merry Wives of Windsor

WHO ☞ *Sir John Falstaff, a fat, lecherous, old knight.*

WHERE ☞ *A room at the Garter Inn, Windsor, c. 1420.*

WHO ELSE IS THERE ☞ *Bardolph, an associate of Falstaff and a tapster (someone who draws ale) at the Garter Inn, is present at the beginning of the speech.*

WHAT HAS JUST HAPPENED ☞ *Having had to escape in a laundry basket from the husband of a woman he is trying to seduce, Falstaff has been thrown into the River Thames.*

WHAT TO THINK ABOUT ☞

- *Falstaff needs a drink.*

- *Think what Falstaff must feel like and look like and how you can present that.*

- *Falstaff could just be talking to himself or telling his story to the audience; perhaps a mixture of the two. Decide where he might shift from one to the other.*

- *Decide whether he is openly seeking sympathy from the audience.*

- *Falstaff has been scared, outraged, humiliated, embarrassed and humbled. These will all affect the way he delivers his speech.*

- *Decide if his drink arrives and if so whether it makes him feel any better.*

WHERE ELSE TO LOOK ☞ *Trinculo (The Tempest, p. 20) is also wet and in conversation with the audience. Benedick (Much Ado About Nothing, p. 32) shares his thoughts with the audience as well.*

## *Falstaff*

**❝** Go fetch me a quart of sack,* put a toast* in't.

*Exit Bardolph.*

Have I lived to be carried in a basket like a barrow of
butcher's offal? And to be thrown in the Thames? Well, if I
be served such another trick, I'll have my brains ta'en out
and buttered, and give them to a dog for a New Year's gift.
The rogues slighted* me into the river with as little remorse
as they would have drowned a blind bitch's puppies,
fifteen i' the litter! And you may know by my size that I have
a kind of alacrity in sinking: if the bottom were as deep as
hell, I should down. I had been drowned, but that the shore
was shelvy* and shallow – a death that I abhor, for the water
swells a man, and what a thing should I have been when I
had been swelled! I should have been a mountain of
mummy.* **❞**

(*Act 3, scene 5, line 3 onwards*)

GLOSSARY

*sack* – dry white wine, probably sherry
*toast* – chaser, garnish
*slighted* – threw
*shelvy* – sloping
*mummy* – pulp

# Measure for Measure

WHO ☞ *Angelo, deputy to the Duke of Vienna who is given full authority in the Duke's absence.*

WHERE ☞ *Angelo's house in Vienna.*

WHO ELSE IS THERE ☞ *Isabel (also called Isabella), a novice from a convent whom Angelo lusts after.*

WHAT IS HAPPENING ☞ *The Duke of Vienna has left Angelo to rule the city in his absence abroad. Angelo has condemned Claudio to death but told his sister Isabel that he will halt the execution if she will sleep with him. Isabel tells Angelo that she will report his threat, but he replies that no one will believe her.*

WHAT TO THINK ABOUT ☞

- *Angelo has power over Isabel. Decide whether he has ever had such power before, how much he enjoys it and whether his new power might also disturb him.*

- *Decide how much of a villain Angelo is and whether there is anything to be done to make him more complex.*

- *The sentence beginning, 'I have begun', might be to himself and out of hearing of Isabel.*

- *Decide why Angelo gives Isabel until the next day to reply and what expectations he has of her reply.*

WHERE ELSE TO LOOK ☞ *Richard (Richard III, p. 78) has another form of power over a woman. Aaron (Titus Andronicus, p. 92) does not have any doubts about his actions.*

## *Angelo*

**❝** Who will believe thee, Isabel?
My unsoil'd name, th'austereness of my life,
My vouch against you,* and my place i'th' state,
Will so your accusation overweigh
That you shall stifle* in your own report
And smell of calumny.* I have begun,
And now I give my sensual race the rein.
Fit thy consent to my sharp appetite,
Lay by all nicety and prolixious* blushes
That banish what they sue for,* redeem thy brother
By yielding up thy body to my will,
Or else he must not only die the death
But thy unkindness shall his death draw out
To lingering sufferance. Answer me tomorrow,
Or, by the affection that now guides me most,
I'll prove a tyrant to him. As for you,
Say what you can, my false o'erweighs your true. **❞**

(*Act 2, scene 4, lines 154–70*)

GLOSSARY

*My vouch against you* – my word against yours
*stifle* – suffocate
*calumny* – lies
*prolixious* – tedious
*banish what they sue for* – have the opposite effect than they intend

# Much Ado About Nothing

WHO ☞ *Benedick, a gentleman.*

WHERE ☞ *The orchard at the house of Leonato, the Governor of Messina, a province of Sicily.*

WHO ELSE IS THERE ☞ *Benedick is alone, a servant boy having just left on an errand.*

WHAT IS HAPPENING ☞ *His best friend Claudio has fallen in love with a girl called Hero. Benedick is amazed that someone who was so against love can so easily fall in love. He swears the same thing will never happen to him.*

WHAT TO THINK ABOUT ☞

- *Benedick needs someone to talk to, so he might 'find' the audience here to share his thoughts.*

- *Picture and dramatise Claudio and the changes that love has made in him.*

- *Decide why Benedick is so adamant that he will never fall in love and whether he really means it.*

- *As he talks of women being fair, wise and virtuous he could refer to individual women in the audience and demonstrate that they do not affect him, or appear to conjure them vividly in his mind's eye.*

- *Decide whether he begins to weaken towards the end as he lists the qualities that will be in the woman he might love.*

- *The last line indicates that he is about to be interrupted by Don Pedro ('The Prince') and Claudio ('Monsieur Love').*

WHERE ELSE TO LOOK ☞ *Richard (Richard III, p. 78) is immune to love though able to get others to love him. Berowne (Love's Labour's Lost, p. 38) once thought he would never fall in love.*

## *Benedick*

**❝** I do much wonder that one man, seeing how much another man is a fool when he dedicates his behaviours to love, will, after he hath laughed at such shallow follies in others, become the argument of his own scorn by falling in love: and such a man is Claudio. I have known when there was no music with him but the drum and the fife* – and now had he rather hear the tabor and the pipe.* I have known when he would have walked ten mile afoot to see a good armour – and now will he lie ten nights awake, carving the fashion of a new doublet. He was wont to* speak plain and to the purpose, like an honest man and a soldier – and now is he turned orthography!* His words are a very fantastical banquet, just so many strange dishes. May I be so converted and see with these eyes? I cannot tell; I think not. I will not be sworn but love may transform me to an oyster – but I'll take my oath on it, till he have made an oyster of me, he shall never make me such a fool. One woman is fair, yet I am well; another is wise, yet I am well; another virtuous, yet I am well. But till all graces be in one woman, one woman shall not come in my grace.* Rich she shall be, that's certain; wise, or I'll none; virtuous, or I'll never cheapen her; fair, or I'll never look on her; mild, or come not near me; noble, or not I for an angel; of good discourse, an excellent musician, and her hair shall be of what colour it please God. – Ha! The Prince and Monsieur Love! I will hide me in the arbour.* **❞**

*(Act 2, scene 3, line 8 onwards)*

GLOSSARY

*the drum and the fife* – instruments of war and soldiery
*the tabor and the pipe* – instruments of love and romance
*was wont to* – used to
*turned orthography* – suddenly started to speak in a fancy way
*grace* – favour
*arbour* – bower, shady retreat

# Much Ado About Nothing

WHO ☞ *Leonato, the governor of Messina, a province of Sicily.*

WHERE ☞ *Outside Leonato's house.*

WHO ELSE IS THERE ☞ *Leonato's brother Antonio.*

WHAT IS HAPPENING ☞ *Leonato's daughter Hero has been wrongly accused of infidelity. Tormented by these accusations, her father Leonato expresses his grief to Antonio, who is trying to comfort him.*

WHAT TO THINK ABOUT ☞

- *Leonato is grief-stricken at his daughter's disgrace.*
- *His grief is a mixture of many emotions which include anger, sorrow, incomprehension, bitterness, rage, and love. Try assigning particular shades of emotion to particular lines.*
- *Decide how these emotions affect his voice and his body.*
- *Work out where these emotions and thoughts are directed, which could be to Antonio, to himself, to the world around or to his disgraced daughter at different times in the speech.*
- *Decide whether the speech ends on a note of exhaustion or rising anger, something else or something in between.*

WHERE ELSE TO LOOK ☞ *Stricken with a different grief are Titus (Titus Andronicus, p. 90) and Pericles (Pericles, p. 54).*

### *Leonato*

**❝** I pray thee, cease thy counsel,
Which falls into mine ears as profitless
As water in a sieve. Give not me counsel,
Nor let no comforter delight mine ear
But such a one whose wrongs do suit with mine.

Bring me a father that so lov'd his child,
Whose joy of her is overwhelm'd like mine,
And bid him speak of patience.
Measure his woe the length and breadth of mine,
And let it answer every strain for strain,
As thus for thus, and such a grief for such,
In every lineament, branch, shape, and form.
If such a one will smile and stroke his beard,
Bid sorrow's wag* cry 'hem' when he should groan,
Patch grief with proverbs, make misfortune drunk
With candle-wasters,* bring him yet to me,
And I of him will gather patience.
But there is no such man: for, brother, men
Can counsel and speak comfort to that grief
Which they themselves not feel; but tasting it,
Their counsel turns to passion, which before
Would give preceptial medicine* to rage,
Fetter strong madness in a silken thread,
Charm ache with air and agony with words.
No, no, 'tis all men's office to speak patience
To those that wring* under the load of sorrow,
But no man's virtue nor sufficiency
To be so moral when he shall endure
The like himself. Therefore give me no counsel.
My griefs cry louder than advertisement.* **99**

*(Act 5, scene 1, lines 3–32)*

GLOSSARY

*sorrow's wag* – the victim of sorrow
*candle-wasters* – those up late at night
*preceptial medicine* – wise instructions
*wring* – struggle
*advertisement* – advice (Leonato is saying that no advice can overcome
   his grief)

# Love's Labour's Lost

WHO ☞ *Don Armado, a fantastical Spaniard.*

WHERE ☞ *A park with a palace in it, in Navarre, now in north-east Spain, then an independent kingdom.*

WHO ELSE IS THERE ☞ *Don Armado is alone.*

WHAT IS HAPPENING ☞ *With his customary Mediterranean excess, the Spaniard Don Armado talks to himself of his love for the country wench Jacquenetta.*

WHAT TO THINK ABOUT ☞

- *Don Armado is Spanish and Shakespeare has fun with his depiction of a flamboyant stereotype. England was at war with Spain when Shakespeare wrote the play.*

- *At first Don Armado tries to resist the notion that he is in love.*

- *Good opportunities for physical comedy here include Don Armado kissing the ground where his love has walked and mock fighting with a rapier.*

- *Enjoy the repetitious quality of some of the phrases.*

- *Decide whether Don Armado has an accent.*

WHERE ELSE TO LOOK ☞ *Other speeches with opportunities for physical comedy include Trinculo (The Tempest, p. 20) and Launce (The Two Gentlemen of Verona, p. 24).*

## Don Armado

**❝** I do affect the very ground, which is base, where her
shoe, which is baser, guided by her foot, which is basest, doth
tread. I shall be forsworn,* which is a great argument of
falsehood, if I love. And how can that be true love which is
falsely attempted? Love is a familiar.* Love is a devil. There
is no evil angel but Love. Yet was Samson* so tempted, and
he had an excellent strength. Yet was Solomon* so seduced,
and he had a very good wit. Cupid's butt-shaft* is too hard
for Hercules' club, and therefore too much odds for a
Spaniard's rapier. The first and second cause will not serve
my turn; the *passado** he respects not, the *duello** he regards
not. His disgrace is to be called boy, but his glory is to
subdue men. Adieu, valour! Rust, rapier! Be still, drum! For
your manager is in love; yea, he loveth. Assist me, some
extemporal god of rhyme, for I am sure I shall turn sonnet.
Devise, wit; write, pen; for I am for whole volumes in
folio. **❞**

(*Act 1, scene 2, line 159 onwards*)

GLOSSARY

*forsworn* – perjured
*familiar* – personal devil
*Samson . . . Solomon* – famous lovers in the Bible, both punished for
    their actions
*Cupid's butt-shaft* – blunt-headed arrow of the god of love
*passado* – thrust from a sword
*duello* – duel

# Love's Labour's Lost

WHO ☞ *Berowne, a lord attending the King of Navarre.*

WHERE ☞ *A park with a palace in it, in Navarre, now in north-east Spain, then an independent kingdom.*

WHO ELSE IS THERE ☞ *Berowne is alone.*

WHAT IS HAPPENING ☞ *Having always mocked others for falling in love, Berowne (pronounced 'Beroon') finds that he has now fallen in love himself.*

WHAT TO THINK ABOUT ☞

- *Berowne begins by declaring how watchful he has been against the visitations of love.*

- *Then he paints a detailed picture of Cupid, the god of love, with a rich, elaborate mix of romantic and sexual images. Make this more than a list but a series of newly thought images each prompted by the one that has gone before.*

- *Then he talks of wives and how they are like German clocks always going wrong. Imagine the type of woman he has in mind.*

- *He despairs that of the three women he and his two friends have met, he has had to fall in love with the least attractive.*

WHERE ELSE TO LOOK ☞ *Benedick (Much Ado About Nothing, p. 32) believes he will never become a victim of love.*

### Berowne

**❝** O, and I forsooth, in love, I that have been love's whip?
A very beadle* to a humorous sigh,
A critic, nay, a night-watch constable,
A domineering pedant o'er the boy,
Than whom no mortal so magnificent!
This wimpled,* whining, purblind,* wayward boy,

This senior-junior, giant-dwarf, Don Cupid,
Regent of love-rhymes, lord of folded arms,
Th'anointed sovereign of sighs and groans,
Liege of all loiterers and malcontents,
Dread prince of plackets,* king of codpieces,*
Sole imperator and great general
Of trotting paritors,* O my little heart!
And I to be a corporal of his field,
And wear his colours like a tumbler's hoop!
What? I love, I sue, I seek a wife?
A woman, that is like a German clock,
Still a-repairing,* ever out of frame,
And never going aright, being a watch,
But being watch'd that it may still go right.
Nay, to be perjured, which is worst of all.
And, among three, to love the worst of all –
A whitely wanton,* with a velvet brow,
With two pitch-balls stuck in her face for eyes.
Ay, and by heaven, one that will do the deed
Though Argus* were her eunuch and her guard:
And I to sigh for her! to watch for her!
To pray for her! Go to; it is a plague
That Cupid will impose for my neglect
Of his almighty dreadful little might.
Well, I will love, write, sigh, pray, sue and groan:
Some men must love my lady and some Joan.* 🙶

(*Act 3, scene 1, lines 169–200*)

GLOSSARY

*beadle* – constable
*wimpled* – blind-folded
*purblind* – half-blind, short-sighted
*plackets* – openings in the front of skirts (revealing what is inside)
*codpieces* – pocket in the front of trousers (displaying what is inside)
*trotting paritors* – puritanical bureaucrats
*still a-repairing* – always needing mending
*whitely wanton* – fair-skinned seducer
*Argus* – a sentry in classical mythology with a hundred eyes
*Joan* – a lower-class woman

# A Midsummer Night's Dream

WHO ☞ *Oberon, King of the Fairies.*

WHERE ☞ *The woods outside Athens.*

WHO ELSE IS THERE ☞ *His servant Puck, who has just been sent to bring back a magic flower.*

WHAT IS HAPPENING ☞ *Puck returns with the magic flower that Oberon has sent him to fetch. Oberon describes the place where his wife Titania is sleeping and how he intends to use the flower to get his revenge on her for stealing a little boy from him. He then sends Puck with some of the flower to make a young man he has seen fall in love with a young woman.*

WHAT TO THINK ABOUT ☞

- *This is a very sensual speech, rich in language, and in rhyming couplets.*

- *Oberon is creating with words the place where Titania is asleep.*

- *Each of the flowers he mentions is real and has different qualities from the others.*

- *Work on every sense through the speech – the smell, taste, look, feel and sound of the bank where Titania is sleeping.*

- *Notice the change of mood when Oberon announces what he intends to do with the flower.*

- *Picture the flower and think what its special qualities are.*

- *In the second half of the speech Oberon tells Puck to find a young man in the woods and use the magic flower to get him to fall in love with a girl, the 'Athenian lady', who is in love with him. Decide why Oberon also uses the flower in this way.*

- *Think about Oberon's relationship with Puck and how it is expressed vocally.*

WHERE ELSE TO LOOK ☞ *Othello's revenge on the wife he thinks to have been unfaithful is more extreme (Othello, p. 116).*

## *Oberon*

**❝** Hast thou the flower there?
I pray thee, give it me.
I know a bank where the wild thyme blows,
Where oxlips and the nodding violet grows,
Quite over-canopied with luscious woodbine,
With sweet musk-roses and with eglantine.
There sleeps Titania sometime of the night,
Lull'd in these flowers with dances and delight;
And there the snake throws her enamell'd* skin,
Weed* wide enough to wrap a fairy in.
And with the juice of this I'll streak her eyes,
And make her full of hateful fantasies.
Take thou some of it, and seek through this grove.
A sweet Athenian lady is in love
With a disdainful youth. Anoint his eyes,
But do it when the next thing he espies
May be the lady. Thou shalt know the man
By the Athenian garments he hath on.
Effect it with some care, that he may prove
More fond on her than she upon her love.
And look thou meet me ere the first cock crow. **❞**

*(Act 2, scene 1, lines 246–66)*

GLOSSARY

*enamell'd* – brightly coloured
*weed* – garment

# A Midsummer Night's Dream

WHO ☞ *Bottom, a weaver.*

WHERE ☞ *The woods outside Athens.*

WHO ELSE IS THERE ☞ *Bottom is alone.*

WHAT IS HAPPENING ☞ *While rehearsing with his fellow workmen for a play to be presented in front of the Duke, Bottom has been transformed by the fairy Puck so that his head has turned into that of a donkey (or ass). Titania, Queen of the Fairies, has been drugged into falling in love with him. Bottom wakes and thinks it has all been a dream.*

WHAT TO THINK ABOUT ☞

- *His first lines are spoken as he emerges from a dream he is having about putting on the play.*

- *Work out the geography of the scene. Decide where Bottom is and how far he goes from the spot he wakes in to search for his companions.*

- *Each of the companions he shouts for is a different person with a different relationship to Bottom.*

- *Decide at what moment he realises that he is alone.*

- *When he says 'methought', he is remembering what he thinks is a dream, when he was an ass with an ass's head but also in love with a beautiful woman professing her love for him. But he still can't bring himself to say the actual words.*

- *Notice how the eye, ear, hand, tongue and heart 'of man' don't quite match up with the verbs Bottom assigns them!*

WHERE ELSE TO LOOK ☞ *Other humorous speeches to the audience are from Launce (The Two Gentlemen of Verona, p. 24) and Benedick (Much Ado About Nothing, p. 32).*

## *Bottom*

*Awaking.*

66 When my cue comes, call me, and I will answer. My next is, 'Most fair Pyramus.' Hey-ho. Peter Quince? Flute the bellows-mender? Snout the tinker? Starveling? God's my life, stolen hence, and left me asleep! I have had a most rare vision. I have had a dream past the wit of man to say what dream it was. Man is but an ass if he go about to expound this dream. Methought I was – there is no man can tell what. Methought I was – and methought I had – but man is but a patched fool* if he will offer to say what methought I had. The eye of man hath not heard, the ear of man hath not seen, man's hand is not able to taste, his tongue to conceive, nor his heart to report, what my dream was. I will get Peter Quince to write a ballad of this dream, it shall be called 'Bottom's Dream', because it hath no bottom. And I will sing it in the latter end of a play, before the Duke. Peradventure, to make it the more gracious, I shall sing it at her death.* 99

(*Act 4, scene 1, line 206 onwards*)

GLOSSARY

*patched fool* – fool wearing motley (clothing made of patches)
*her death* – the death of the character Thisbe in the play that was being rehearsed

# The Merchant of Venice

WHO ☞ *Shylock, a Jewish money-lender.*

WHERE ☞ *A street in Venice.*

WHO ELSE IS THERE ☞ *Antonio, the merchant of the play's title, and his friend Bassanio.*

WHAT IS HAPPENING ☞ *Bassanio wants money so as to be able to impress the girl he is in love with. His friend Antonio has asked Shylock to lend him money so that he might give it to Bassanio. The Jew expresses his disbelief that he should be expected to lend money to someone who has been so abusive to him in the past.*

WHAT TO THINK ABOUT ☞

- *Play with the issues of status in this speech. Shylock has been treated badly by the man who now needs his help.*

- *Shylock is at times bitter, sarcastic, angry, vengeful, humorous and patronising. Work out how to play these different attitudes.*

- *Think what responses Shylock expects or hopes for.*

- *Decide whether he gives Antonio space to reply and whether he pauses sarcastically between his questions.*

- *The speech has the three strong monosyllabic words, 'Go to then', in the middle. Deliver them strongly.*

WHERE ELSE TO LOOK ☞ *Other characters with a grievance include the Duke of York (Richard II, p. 60) and Iago (Othello, p. 114).*

## *Shylock*

**❝** Signior Antonio, many a time and oft
In the Rialto* you have rated* me
About my moneys and my usances.*
Still have I borne it with a patient shrug,
For sufferance is the badge of all our tribe.
You call me misbeliever, cut-throat dog,
And spit upon my Jewish gaberdine,*
And all for use of that which is mine own.
Well then, it now appears you need my help.
Go to then.* You come to me, and you say
'Shylock, we would have moneys,' you say so.
You, that did void your rheum* upon my beard,
And foot me as you spurn a stranger cur*
Over your threshold. Moneys is your suit.
What should I say to you? Should I not say,
'Hath a dog money? Is it possible
A cur can lend three thousand ducats?' Or
Shall I bend low and in a bondman's key,*
With bated breath and whispering humbleness,
Say this: 'Fair sir, you spat on me on Wednesday last;
You spurn'd me such a day; another time
You call'd me dog; and for these courtesies
I'll lend you thus much moneys'? **❞**

*(Act 1, scene 3, lines 105–27)*

GLOSSARY

*Rialto* – the commercial exchange in Venice
*rated* – berated
*usances* – interests on loans
*gaberdine* – cloak
*Go to then* – enough of that or go away
*void your rheum* – spit
*cur* – dog
*bondman's key* – the voice of a slave

# As You Like It

WHO ☞  *Jaques, a Lord attending Duke Senior who has been banished and is living in exile in the forest.*

WHERE ☞  *The Forest of Arden, named after a forest of the same name in North Warwickshire, near Stratford.*

WHO ELSE IS THERE ☞  *The Duke and others.*

WHAT IS HAPPENING ☞  *The famously melancholy Jaques (usually pronounced 'Jay-quez') is living, somewhat reluctantly, with Duke Senior and other members of the Duke's retinue in the forest. He finds the Duke to tell him that he has just met a fool in the forest dressed in motley, the multi-coloured clothing of a jester.*

WHAT TO THINK ABOUT ☞

- *There is an urgency and breathlessness about the opening of the speech.*

- *Jaques can hardly get his words out at the beginning, and it is a while before his language settles down and the verse becomes regular.*

- *He has been excited by meeting a fool who has talked comically about the nature of time.*

- *Create the character of the fool as Jaques talks about him. Think what his voice and mannerisms are like. Try to see him as Jaques would in his mind's eye.*

- *With three short three- and four-word sentences the speech comes to a slow, strong conclusion very different from its opening.*

WHERE ELSE TO LOOK ☞  *Don Armado (Love's Labour's Lost, p. 36) gives another verbally flamboyant speech. Launce (The Two Gentlemen of Verona, p. 24) also acts out a scene he has witnessed.*

## *Jaques*

**❝** A fool, a fool! I met a fool i'th' forest,
A motley fool – a miserable world! -
As I do live by food, I met a fool,
Who laid him down and bask'd him in the sun,
And rail'd on* Lady Fortune in good terms,
In good set terms, and yet a motley fool.
'Good morrow, fool,' quoth I. 'No, sir,' quoth he,
'Call me not fool till heaven hath sent me fortune.'
And then he drew a dial* from his poke,*
And, looking on it with lack-lustre eye,
Says very wisely, 'It is ten o'clock.
Thus we may see,' quoth he, 'how the world wags.*
'Tis but an hour ago since it was nine,
And after one hour more 'twill be eleven;
And so from hour to hour we ripe and ripe,
And then from hour to hour we rot and rot,
And thereby hangs a tale.' When I did hear
The motley fool thus moral on the time,
My lungs began to crow like Chanticleer,*
That fools should be so deep-contemplative,
And I did laugh, sans* intermission,
An hour by his dial. O noble fool!
A worthy fool! Motley's the only wear. **❞**

(*Act 2, scene 7, lines 12–34*)

GLOSSARY

*rail'd on* – was abusive to, verbally abused
*dial* – watch
*poke* – pocket
*wags* – goes
*Chanticleer* – rooster
*sans* – without

# The Taming of the Shrew

WHO ☞ *Petruchio, a gentleman of Verona, newly married to Katharina.*

WHERE ☞ *A room in Petruchio's house in the countryside outside Verona.*

WHO ELSE IS THERE ☞ *Petruchio is alone.*

WHAT IS HAPPENING ☞ *Having married Katharina who had a reputation as being wilful and ungovernable (the 'shrew' of the play's title) Petruchio is now 'taming' her the way men train wild hawks. He is depriving her of food and sleep and constantly finding fault in order to break her will and make her an obedient wife.*

WHAT TO THINK ABOUT ☞

- *Petruchio is reporting to the audience on how his 'taming' is progressing. Decide how difficult this is proving and whether he is exultant at his success or exhausted by the difficulty of his task.*

- *Decide why he refers to hawking. Perhaps Petruchio is a successful hawksman. Perhaps Katharina is as dangerous as a wild hawk.*

- *The plan about the bed may be one that Petruchio thinks up as he is talking to the audience or it could be that he has already decided on it.*

- *When he asks 'he that knows better' to speak out, decide whether he is genuinely asking for help from the audience, or boasting that he knows best.*

WHERE ELSE TO LOOK ☞ *Also talking to the audience about women are Benedick (Much Ado About Nothing, p. 32) and Richard (Richard III, p. 78).*

## *Petruchio*

**❝** Thus have I politicly* begun my reign,
And 'tis my hope to end successfully.
My falcon now is sharp and passing empty,*
And till she stoop,* she must not be full-gorged,*
For then she never looks upon her lure.*
Another way I have to man my haggard,*
To make her come, and know her keeper's call,
That is, to watch her, as we watch these kites*
That bate,* and beat, and will not be obedient.
She ate no meat today, nor none shall eat.
Last night she slept not, nor to-night she shall not.
As with the meat, some undeservèd fault
I'll find about the making of the bed,
And here I'll fling the pillow, there the bolster,
This way the coverlet, another way the sheets.
Ay, and amid this hurly I intend
That all is done in reverend care of her.
And in conclusion she shall watch all night,
And if she chance to nod I'll rail* and brawl,
And with the clamour keep her still awake.
This is a way to kill a wife with kindness,
And thus I'll curb her mad and headstrong humour.
He that knows better how to tame a shrew,
Now let him speak, 'tis charity to show. **❞**

(*Act 4, scene 1, lines 173–96*)

GLOSSARY

*politicly* – cleverly, carefully, cunningly
*passing empty* – very hungry
*stoop* – submit, swoop on prey
*full-gorged* – fully fed
*lure* – in falconry a device to bring back a hawk
*man my haggard* – tame my wild hawk
*kites* – wild hawk
*bate* – flutter
*rail* – rant, rail, be abusive

# Twelfth Night

WHO ☞ *Sebastian, a young gentleman.*

WHERE ☞ *The garden of the countess Olivia, in Illyria, a semi-mythical place on the coast of present-day Croatia.*

WHO ELSE IS THERE ☞ *Sebastian is alone.*

WHAT IS HAPPENING ☞ *Viola and her twin brother Sebastian have been shipwrecked and both think the other has perished. The Countess Olivia has fallen in love with Viola who is dressed as a boy. When she sees Sebastian, Olivia thinks that he is the disguised Viola and is at last able to make love to him. Afterwards, Sebastian is so surprised by what has occurred that he thinks either he or Olivia must be mad.*

WHAT TO THINK ABOUT ☞

* *Sebastian is disbelieving of what has just happened.*

* *His first phrase, 'This is the air', is full of possibilities: he has just come outside, is breathing fresh air, has escaped from the house, is back in the real world and so surely cannot be mad.*

* *Decide how worried Sebastian is that he might really be mad and how unbelievable what has just happened to him seems.*

* *Antonio is his only friend in Illyria.*

* *Decide what his thoughts are about Olivia and build up a picture of her in your mind.*

* *Decide what his reaction is when he sees her coming out of the house towards him at the end of his speech.*

WHERE ELSE TO LOOK ☞ *Other monologues about falling in love which can be played to the audience include Proteus (The Two Gentlemen of Verona, p. 22) and Benedick (Much Ado About Nothing, p. 32).*

## *Sebastian*

**❝** This is the air, that is the glorious sun,
This pearl she gave me, I do feel't and see't,
And though 'tis wonder that enwraps me thus,
Yet 'tis not madness. Where's Antonio then?
I could not find him at the Elephant,*
Yet there he was,* and there I found this credit,*
That he did range the town to seek me out.
His counsel now might do me golden service,
For though my soul disputes well with my sense
That this may be some error, but no madness,
Yet doth this accident and flood of fortune*
So far exceed all instance, all discourse,
That I am ready to distrust mine eyes,
And wrangle with my reason that persuades me
To any other trust but that I am mad,
Or else the lady's mad. Yet, if 'twere so,
She could not sway* her house, command her followers,
Take and give back affairs, and their dispatch,
With such a smooth, discreet, and stable bearing
As I perceive she does. There's something in't
That is deceivable.* But here the lady comes. **❞**

*(Act 4, scene 3, lines 1–21)*

GLOSSARY

*Elephant* – a pub of that name (possibly a jokey reference to a real pub not far from the Globe Theatre)
*was* – had been
*credit* – news
*this accident and flood of fortune* – i.e. his chance meeting with Olivia and her showering him with gifts
*sway* – maintain order over
*deceivable* – deceptive

# The Winter's Tale

WHO ☞ *An old Shepherd.*

WHERE ☞ *Deserted countryside by the sea in Bohemia.*

WHO ELSE IS THERE ☞ *A baby which the shepherd does not at first see.*

WHAT IS HAPPENING ☞ *Lord Antigonus has been ordered by the King to kill the newborn baby princess but cannot bear to do so. Instead he abandons her on the beach before being chased off by a bear. A shepherd then enters and finds the baby whom he names Perdita, meaning the lost one.*

WHAT TO THINK ABOUT ☞

- *The shepherd is looking for a lost sheep.*

- *Imagine the environment and decide how loudly he has to shout to be heard in the bad weather.*

- *The part would probably have been written for a clown in Shakespeare's company. There are strong comic possibilities in the realisation of finding a baby.*

- *There are also comic possibilities in his trying to find out the baby's sex.*

- *Think about his relationship with his son and why he decides to wait for him.*

WHERE ELSE TO LOOK ☞ *Trinculo (The Tempest, p. 20) also finds something on the ground by the sea in the rain.*

## *Shepherd*

**❝** I would there were no age between ten and three-and-twenty, or that youth would sleep out the rest, for there is nothing in the between but getting wenches with child, wronging the ancientry,* stealing, fighting. Hark you now! Would any but these boiled brains* of nineteen, and two-and-twenty hunt this weather? They have scared away two of my best sheep, which I fear the wolf will sooner find than the master: if anywhere I have them, 'tis by the seaside, browsing* of ivy. Good luck, an't be thy will, what have we here! Mercy on's, a bairn, a very pretty bairn! A boy or a child, I wonder? A pretty one; a very pretty one. Sure, some 'scape.* Though I am not bookish, yet I can read waiting-gentlewoman in the 'scape. This has been some stair-work, some trunk-work, some behind-door-work. They were warmer that got this than the poor thing is here. I'll take it up for pity, yet I'll tarry till my son come. He hallooed but even now. Whoa, ho, hoa! **❞**

*(Act 3, scene 3, line 58 onwards)*

GLOSSARY

*ancientry* – old people
*boiled brains* – hotheads
*browsing* – grazing
*'scape* – sexual escapade (he is sure the baby is the result of an illicit affair with a female servant)

# Pericles

WHO ☞ *Pericles, exiled Prince of Tyre.*

WHERE ☞ *On board a ship at sea in ancient times.*

WHO ELSE IS THERE ☞ *The nurse Lychorida and sailors.*

WHAT IS HAPPENING ☞ *In a storm at sea, Pericles' wife Thaisa has just died while giving birth to their daughter Marina. Pericles sees his child for the first time while saying farewell to his dead wife.*

WHAT TO THINK ABOUT ☞

- *Pericles has to deal with both his own emotions and the practicalities of birth and death.*

- *His first lines are addressed to his dead wife.*

- *He is on a ship at sea in a storm that is threatening to kill everyone on board.*

- *His wife has died in childbirth so he is feeling both grief and joy.*

- *He must prepare his wife for immediate burial at sea; the sailors have told him her body is bringing bad luck.*

- *He must care for his newborn child, whom he is holding for the first time.*

- *Emotion might explode from him in the last two lines of the speech as he calls to the nurse.*

WHERE ELSE TO LOOK ☞ *Leonato (Much Ado About Nothing, p. 34) grieves for his daughter's reputation and Titus (Titus Andronicus, p. 90) for what has happened to his daughter.*

## *Pericles*

**66** A terrible childbed hast thou had, my dear;
No light, no fire. The unfriendly elements
Forgot thee utterly. Nor have I time
To give thee hallow'd* to thy grave, but straight
Must cast thee, scarcely coffin'd, in the ooze,*
Where, for a monument upon thy bones,
And e'er-remaining lamps, the belching whale
And humming water must o'erwhelm thy corpse,
Lying with simple shells. O Lychorida,
Bid Nestor* bring me spices, ink and paper,
My casket and my jewels; and bid Nicander*
Bring me the satin coffer. Lay the babe
Upon the pillow. Hie thee, whiles I say
A priestly farewell to her. Suddenly,* woman. **99**

*(Act 3, scene 1, lines 57–70)*

GLOSSARY

*hallow'd* – blessed
*ooze* – bottom of the sea
*e'er-remaining lamps* – memorial candles
*Nestor . . . Nicander* – names of servants
*suddenly* – quickly

# The Histories

# King John

WHO ☞    *Lewis the Dauphin (eldest son of the King) of France.*

WHERE ☞    *The French camp near Bury St Edmund's, c. 1216.*

WHO ELSE IS THERE ☞    *The Earls of Salisbury, Norfolk and Pembroke, Melun a French Lord, Cardinal Pandulph and others.*

WHAT IS HAPPENING ☞    *Cardinal Pandulph comes from the Pope, to tell Lewis that the Pope has made his peace with King John and that he must end his war with England. Having been encouraged by the Pope to make war in the first place, the Dauphin vents his anger on the Cardinal.*

WHAT TO THINK ABOUT ☞

- *This is a public speech. The court is waiting to hear what Lewis has to say.*

- *He keeps them waiting for a moment with his first polite few words addressed to Cardinal Pandulph.*

- *Then come four strong and simple monosyllabic words: 'I will not back.'*

- *Lewis has two audiences. One is Cardinal Pandulph, and through him the Pope, the other is his court and soldiers. Be clear as to which points are being made to which audience.*

- *Lewis is a leader winning a war. This will affect him physically and vocally. But he has been thwarted by the Pope's interference, which makes him very angry and indignant.*

- *The last line almost has the beat of a war drum behind it.*

WHERE ELSE TO LOOK ☞    *Henry (Henry V, p. 68) also has to respond publicly to an attempted humiliation.*

## *Lewis the Dauphin*

**❝** Your grace shall pardon me, I will not back.
I am too high-born to be propertied\*
To be a secondary at control,

Or useful serving-man and instrument
To any sovereign state throughout the world.
Your breath first kindled the dead coal of wars
Between this chastis'd kingdom and myself,
And brought in matter that should feed this fire;
And now 'tis far too huge to be blown out
With that same weak wind which enkindled it.
You taught me how to know the face of right,
Acquainted me with interest to this land,
Yea, thrust this enterprise into my heart,
And come ye now to tell me John hath made
His peace with Rome? What is that peace to me?
I, by the honour of my marriage-bed,
After young Arthur,* claim this land for mine,
And, now it is half-conquer'd, must I back,
Because that John hath made his peace with Rome?
Am I Rome's slave? What penny hath Rome borne,
What men provided, what munition sent,
To underprop this action? Is't not I
That undergo this charge? Who else but I,
And such as to my claim are liable,
Sweat in this business, and maintain this war?
Have I not heard these islanders shout out
'Vive le roi!'* as I have bank'd their towns?
Have I not here the best cards for the game
To win this easy match, play'd for a crown?
And shall I now give o'er the yielded set?
No, no, on my soul, it never shall be said. 🙙

(*Act 5, scene 2, lines 78–108*)

GLOSSARY

*propertied* – taken control of
*young Arthur* – English Prince who has been usurped by King John and
    on whose side the French are fighting
*Vive le roi!* – (French) Long live the King!

# Richard II

WHO ☞ *The Duke of York.*

WHERE ☞ *A room in Ely House, London, near present-day Holborn Circus, 1399.*

WHO ELSE IS THERE ☞ *The King, the Queen, the Earl of Northumberland, Lords Ross and Willoughby and others.*

WHAT IS HAPPENING ☞ *The Duke of York and John of Gaunt are brothers, and uncles to the King. Northumberland has just brought word that John of Gaunt is dead. King Richard has said that all his land and possessions must be seized for the crown. The Duke of York's patience with Richard finally runs out and he rebukes the King.*

WHAT TO THINK ABOUT ☞

- *Rebuking a King is not something done lightly, even if he is your nephew.*

- *York is making his rebuke with others present.*

- *There is grief and outrage in the speech.*

- *It is also a speech about family.*

- *Decide whether York regrets what he has said by the end of his speech.*

WHERE ELSE TO LOOK ☞ *Leonato (Much Ado About Nothing, p. 34) is also torn with grief and Shylock (The Merchant of Venice, p. 44) is fierce in his rebukes.*

## Duke of York

**"** O my liege,
Pardon me, if you please; if not, I, pleased
Not to be pardon'd, am content withal.
Seek you to seize and grip into your hands
The royalties and rights of banish'd Hereford?*
Is not Gaunt dead, and doth not Hereford live?
Was not Gaunt just, and is not Harry* true?
Did not the one deserve to have an heir?
Is not his heir a well-deserving son?
Take Hereford's rights away, and take from Time
His charters and his customary rights;
Let not tomorrow then ensue today;
Be not thyself; for how art thou a king
But by fair sequence and succession?
Now, afore God – God forbid I say true! -
If you do wrongfully seize Hereford's rights,
Call in the letters patent that he hath
By his attorneys-general to sue
His livery, and deny his offer'd homage,
You pluck a thousand dangers on your head,
You lose a thousand well-disposèd hearts
And prick my tender patience to those thoughts
Which honour and allegiance cannot think. **"**

(*Act 2, scene 1, lines 187–209*)

GLOSSARY

*Hereford . . . Harry* – Henry Bolingbroke, Duke of Hereford, son of
Gaunt

# Richard II

WHO ☞    *King Richard.*

WHERE ☞    *Flint Castle in Wales, c. 1400.*

WHO ELSE IS THERE ☞    *The Earl of Northumberland, the Duke of York, the Bishop of Carlisle, the Earl of Salisbury and many others. Henry Bolingbroke, Duke of Hereford, is close by.*

WHAT IS HAPPENING ☞    *Besieged in Flint Castle by rebel forces, Richard comes out to listen to the peace terms offered by Northumberland on behalf of the rebel Henry Bolingbroke (later to become King Henry IV). He expresses amazement that Northumberland is not kneeling in his presence.*

WHAT TO THINK ABOUT ☞

- *Richard waits 'thus long' for Northumberland to kneel.*

- *All is at stake for Richard and this is his last chance to face down the rebellion.*

- *He has to be strong and regal and show the highest possible status.*

- *He believes he has God on his side.*

- *He believes his nemesis Bolingbroke to be close by; perhaps in earshot.*

WHERE ELSE TO LOOK ☞    *Lewis (King John, p. 58) and Henry (Henry V, p. 68) both show public strength to political adversaries.*

## *King Richard*

**❝** We are amaz'd, and thus long have we stood
To watch the fearful bending of thy knee
Because we thought ourself thy lawful king;
And if we be, how dare thy joints forget
To pay their awful duty to our presence?
If we be not, show us the hand of God
That hath dismiss'd us from our stewardship,
For well we know, no hand of blood and bone
Can grip the sacred handle of our sceptre
Unless he do profane, steal, or usurp.
And though you think that all, as you have done,
Have torn their souls by turning them from us,
And we are barren and bereft of friends,
Yet know my master, God omnipotent,
Is mustering in His clouds on our behalf
Armies of pestilence, and they shall strike
Your children yet unborn and unbegot,
That lift your vassal\* hands against my head
And threat\* the glory of my precious crown.
Tell Bolingbroke (for yond methinks he is)
That every stride he makes upon my land
Is dangerous treason. He is come to ope
The purple testament\* of bleeding war;
But ere the crown he looks for live in peace,
Ten thousand bloody crowns of mothers' sons
Shall ill become the flower of England's face,
Change the complexion of her maid-pale peace
To scarlet indignation and bedew\*
Her pastures' grass with faithful English blood. **❞**

*(Act 3, scene 3, lines 72–100)*

GLOSSARY

*vassal* – subservient
*threat* – threaten
*purple testament* – blood-stained legacy
*bedew* – make wet with

# Henry IV, Part One

WHO ☞ *Henry 'Hotspur' Percy, son of the Earl of Northumberland and later rebel to King Henry.*

WHERE ☞ *The King's Palace in London, c. 1400.*

WHO ELSE IS THERE ☞ *King Henry, the Earls of Northumberland and Worcester and others.*

WHAT IS HAPPENING ☞ *The King has accused Hotspur of refusing to surrender up his prisoners. Hotspur defends himself and says he acted in anger at the attitude of the lord who came for the prisoners on the King's behalf.*

WHAT TO THINK ABOUT ☞

- *Hotspur has been rebuked by the King but recovers magnificently.*

- *He has just come back from an important military victory.*

- *He tells a story both to the King but also to all the others present.*

- *Here he mocks the voice and mannerisms of the effeminate 'certain lord'. No doubt all in his audience will know the person he is talking about.*

WHERE ELSE TO LOOK ☞ *Petruchio (The Taming of the Shrew, p. 48) has a flamboyant speech to the audience in the theatre.*

## Hotspur

**❝** My liege, I did deny no prisoners;
But I remember, when the fight was done,
When I was dry with rage and extreme toil,
Breathless and faint, leaning upon my sword,
Came there a certain lord, neat and trimly dress'd,
Fresh as a bridegroom, and his chin new reap'd
Show'd like a stubble-land at harvest-home.
He was perfumèd like a milliner,*
And 'twixt his finger and his thumb he held
A pouncet-box,* which ever and anon
He gave his nose and took't away again.
And, as the soldiers bore dead bodies by,
He call'd them untaught knaves, unmannerly,
To bring a slovenly unhandsome corpse
Betwixt the wind and his nobility.
With many holiday and lady terms
He question'd me, amongst the rest demanded
My prisoners in your majesty's behalf.
I then, all smarting with my wounds being cold,
To be so pester'd with a popinjay,*
Out of my grief and my impatience,
Answer'd neglectingly I know not what,
He should or he should not – for he made me mad
To see him shine so brisk, and smell so sweet,
And talk so like a waiting-gentlewoman
Of guns, and drums, and wounds, God save the mark!
This bald unjointed chat of his, my lord,
I answer'd indirectly, as I said,
And I beseech you, let not his report
Come current for an accusation
Betwixt my love and your high majesty. **❞**

*(Act 1, scene 3, lines 29–69, with some cuts)*

GLOSSARY

*milliner* – purveyor of luxury goods
*pouncet-box* – box for snuff or perfume, pomander
*popinjay* – chatterer

# Henry IV, Part Two

WHO ☞ *King Henry.*

WHERE ☞ *A room in the Palace of Westminster, c. 1400.*

WHO ELSE IS THERE ☞ *The King is alone, having just sent for the Earls of Warwick and Surrey.*

WHAT IS HAPPENING ☞ *King Henry is fighting a rebellion. Awake while his subjects sleep, he reflects on the responsibilities of office.*

WHAT TO THINK ABOUT ☞

- *The King cannot sleep. The more he worries about it the less sleep comes.*

- *He creates images of a world in which the lowliest of his subjects can sleep peacefully – even a ship-boy high up in the crow's nest.*

- *Think what it is about being King that sets him apart from all other people and the worries that keep him awake.*

WHERE ELSE TO LOOK ☞ *Macbeth (Macbeth, pp. 102 and 104) and Claudius (Hamlet, p. 106) are other kings alone with their thoughts.*

## *King Henry*

**"** How many thousand of my poorest subjects
Are at this hour asleep! O sleep, O gentle sleep,
Nature's soft nurse, how have I frighted thee,
That thou no more wilt weigh my eyelids down
And steep my senses in forgetfulness?
Why rather, sleep, liest thou in smoky cribs,
Upon uneasy pallets stretching thee,
And hush'd with buzzing night-flies to thy slumber,
Than in the perfumed chambers of the great,
Under the canopies of costly state,
And lull'd with sound of sweetest melody?
O thou dull god, why liest thou with the vile
In loathsome beds, and leav'st the kingly couch
A watch-case or a common 'larum-bell?*
Wilt thou upon the high and giddy mast
Seal up the ship-boy's eyes, and rock his brains
In cradle of the rude imperious* surge,
And in the visitation of the winds,
Who take the ruffian billows by the top,
Curling their monstrous heads and hanging them
With deafening clamour in the slippery clouds,
That, with the hurly, death itself awakes?
Canst thou, O partial sleep, give thy repose
To the wet sea-boy in an hour so rude,
And in the calmest and most stillest night,
With all appliances and means to boot,
Deny it to a king? Then happy low, lie down!
Uneasy lies the head that wears a crown. **"**

*(Act 3, scene 1, lines 5–32)*

GLOSSARY

*leav'st the kingly couch / A watch-case or a common 'larum-bell –*
    transform a royal bed into a ticking watch or loud alarm clock
*imperious* – majestic

# Henry V

WHO ☞ *King Henry.*

WHERE ☞ *A room in the Palace of Westminster, c. 1413.*

WHO ELSE IS THERE ☞ *The Dukes of Gloucester, Bedford and Exeter, the Earls of Warwick and Westmoreland, the Archbishop of Canterbury, the Bishop of Ely, the French Ambassador and others.*

WHAT IS HAPPENING ☞ *Ambassadors arrive from the French Dauphin (eldest son of the King) with a box of tennis balls, saying Henry should stay at home and play games rather than dare to fight for the disputed crown of France. Henry responds with a declaration of war.*

WHAT TO THINK ABOUT ☞

- *Henry has just become King. This speech is his first opportunity to demonstrate his fitness for kingship. He refers to the 'wild days' of his youth.*

- *He has two audiences: the French Dauphin through the ambassadors, and the English court. Use the speech to play to them both.*

- *There is a lightness and humour about the early part of the speech that develops into threats of war. It is possible that Henry grows into the role of King and the status that accompanies it during this speech.*

WHERE ELSE TO LOOK ☞ *Lewis (King John, p. 58) is defiant to an ambassador of a foreign power in the presence of his court.*

## King Henry

**❝** We are glad the Dauphin is so pleasant with us.
His present and your pains we thank you for.
When we have match'd our rackets to these balls,
We will in France, by God's grace, play a set

Shall strike his father's crown into the hazard.*
Tell him he hath made a match with such a wrangler*
That all the courts of France will be disturb'd
With chases.* And we understand him well,
How he comes o'er us with our wilder days,
Not measuring what use we made of them.
We never valued this poor seat of England,
And therefore, living hence, did give ourself
To barbarous licence – as 'tis ever common
That men are merriest when they are from home.
But tell the Dauphin I will keep my state,
Be like a king, and show my sail of greatness,
When I do rouse me in my throne of France.
For that I have laid by my majesty,
And plodded like a man for working-days,
But I will rise there with so full a glory
That I will dazzle all the eyes of France –
Yea, strike the Dauphin blind to look on us.
And tell the pleasant Prince, this mock of his
Hath turn'd his balls to gun-stones, and his soul
Shall stand sore chargèd for the wasteful vengeance
That shall fly with them. For many a thousand widows
Shall this, his mock, mock out of their dear husbands,
Mock mothers from their sons, mock castles down,
And some are yet ungotten and unborn
That shall have cause to curse the Dauphin's scorn.
But this lies all within the will of God,
To whom I do appeal, and in whose name
Tell you the Dauphin I am coming on
To venge me as I may, and to put forth
My rightful hand in a well-hallow'd* cause. 🙶

*(Act 1, scene 2, lines 259–93)*

GLOSSARY

*hazard* – danger (also a term from 'real' tennis and so an image of the
crown being used as a ball in a game)
*wrangler* – opponent
*chases* – pursuit (also the points won in real tennis)
*well-hallow'd* – well-blessed

# Henry V

WHO ☞  *A young boy in service to cowards and thieves.*

WHERE ☞  *Near Harfleur, France, c. 1414.*

WHO ELSE IS THERE ☞  *The boy is alone.*

WHAT IS HAPPENING ☞  *There is about to be a major battle between the English and the French. Hoping soon to leave their service, the boy talks of the cowardice and dishonesty of the soldiers Bardolph, Pistol and Nym, cronies of the dissolute Sir John Falstaff.*

WHAT TO THINK ABOUT ☞

- *This is a turning point for the boy, almost a coming-of-age speech. He has decided to move on.*

- *Try to have a picture of Bardolph, Pistol and Nym in your mind.*

- *Decide how he talks to the audience – perhaps as equals, as confidants or as people to be entertained.*

- *There is an accent of some sort here, indicated by the use of 'a' in place of 'he'. Decide on one you are confident with.*

- *Is the end of the speech the very moment the boy moves on in his life or is it the moment that he realises that he must?*

WHERE ELSE TO LOOK ☞  *Launce (The Two Gentlemen of Verona, p. 24) is another character of low status with something to tell the audience.*

## *Young Boy*

**❝** As young as I am, I have observed these three swashers.*
I am boy to them all three, but all they three, though they
would serve me, could not be man to me, for indeed three
such antiques* do not amount to a man. For Bardolph, he is
white-livered and red-faced, by the means whereof 'a faces it
out, but fights not. For Pistol, he hath a killing tongue and a
quiet sword, by the means whereof 'a breaks words, and
keeps whole weapons. For Nym, he hath heard that men of
few words are the best men, and therefore he scorns to say
his prayers, lest 'a should be thought a coward – but his few
bad words are matched with as few good deeds, for 'a never
broke any man's head but his own, and that was against a
post when he was drunk. They will steal anything, and call it
'purchase'. Bardolph stole a lute-case, bore it twelve leagues,
and sold it for three halfpence. Nym and Bardolph are sworn
brothers in filching,* and in Calais they stole a fire-shovel. I
knew by that piece of service the men would carry coals.*
They would have me as familiar with men's pockets as their
gloves or their handkerchiefs, which makes much against my
manhood if I should take from another's pocket to put into
mine, for it is plain pocketing up of wrongs. I must leave
them, and seek some better service. Their villainy goes
against my weak stomach, and therefore I must cast it up. **❞**

*(Act 3, scene 2, line 27 onwards)*

GLOSSARY

*swashers* – braggarts, boasters
*antiques* – crazy old fools
*filching* – stealing
*carry coals* – show cowardice

# Henry V

WHO ☞ *The Constable of France, a high-ranking officer in the French army.*

WHERE ☞ *The French camp before the decisive battle of Agincourt in France, October 1415.*

WHO ELSE IS THERE ☞ *The Dauphin (eldest son of the King) of France, the Duke of Orleans and others.*

WHAT IS HAPPENING ☞ *The Constable of France urges the French nobles into battle telling them to behold the pathetic English forces ranged against them.*

WHAT TO THINK ABOUT ☞

- *This is a battle-stirring speech.*

- *There is urgency in the Constable's words.*

- *He contrasts the strengths of the 'gallant' French with the weaknesses of the 'sickly' English enemy.*

- *There are two very long sentences followed by the short, rhetorical 'What's to say?' He believes there is nothing to be said in contradiction to him.*

- *There is a rousing rhyming couplet at the end of the speech.*

WHERE ELSE TO LOOK ☞ *Other speeches exhorting armies in battle come from Henry (Henry V, p. 74), Richmond (Richard III, p. 80) and Richard (Richard III, p. 82).*

## *Constable*

**❝** To horse, you gallant princes, straight to horse!
Do but behold yond poor and starvèd band,
And your fair show shall suck away their souls,
Leaving them but the shales* and husks of men.
There is not work enough for all our hands,
Scarce blood enough in all their sickly veins
To give each naked curtle-axe* a stain
That our French gallants shall today draw out,
And sheathe for lack of sport. Let us but blow on them,
The vapour of our valour will o'erturn them.
'Tis positive 'gainst all exceptions, lords,
That our superfluous lackeys and our peasants,
Who in unnecessary action swarm
About our squares of battle, were enough
To purge this field of such a hilding* foe,
Though we upon this mountain's basis by
Took stand for idle speculation,
But that our honours must not. What's to say?
A very little little let us do.
And all is done. Then let the trumpets sound
The tucket sonance* and the note to mount,
For our approach shall so much dare the field
That England shall couch down in fear, and yield. **❞**

*(Act 4, scene 2, lines 15–37)*

GLOSSARY

*shales* – shells
*curtle-axe* – cutlass
*hilding* – worthless
*the tucket sonance* – the sound of a flourish on the trumpet

# Henry V

WHO ☞ *King Henry.*

WHERE ☞ *The English camp before the decisive battle of Agincourt in France, October 1415.*

WHO ELSE IS THERE ☞ *The Dukes of Gloucester, Bedford and Exeter, Sir Thomas Erpingham 'with all his host', and the Earls of Salisbury and Westmoreland.*

WHAT IS HAPPENING ☞ *Before the Battle of Agincourt Henry encourages his men with the thought that because they are fewer in number than their enemy, their victory will be all the greater.*

WHAT TO THINK ABOUT ☞

- *Henry enters to overhear Westmoreland wishing that they had more men from England with them, which means the first few lines are addressed to him.*
- *He has not planned to make a speech.*
- *Work through Henry's thought process as each idea sparks another.*
- *The speech starts with a real question and develops as conversation.*
- *By the end he is exhorting all his troops into battle.*
- *Find a reality for each of the people that he talks about.*

WHERE ELSE TO LOOK ☞ *Other exhortations to battle come from the Constable of France (Henry V, p. 72), Richmond (Richard III, p. 80) and Richard (Richard III, p. 82).*

## King Henry

**66** No, faith, my coz,* wish not a man from England:
God's peace! I would not lose so great an honour
As one man more, methinks, would share from me,
For the best hope I have. O, do not wish one more.
Rather proclaim it, Westmoreland, through my host,

That he which hath no stomach to this fight,
Let him depart. His passport shall be made,
And crowns for convoy* put into his purse.
We would not die in that man's company
That fears his fellowship to die with us.
This day is called the feast of Crispian.*
He that outlives this day, and comes safe home,
Will stand a-tiptoe when this day is nam'd,
And rouse him at the name of Crispian.
He that shall see this day, and live old age,
Will yearly on the vigil feast his neighbours,
And say 'Tomorrow is Saint Crispian.'
Then will he strip his sleeve and show his scars
And say 'These wounds I had on Crispin's day.'
Old men forget; yet all shall be forgot,
But he'll remember with advantages
What feats he did that day. Then shall our names,
Familiar in his mouth as household words –
Harry the King, Bedford and Exeter,
Warwick and Talbot, Salisbury and Gloucester –
Be in their flowing cups freshly remember'd.
This story shall the good man teach his son,
And Crispin Crispian shall ne'er go by,
From this day to the ending of the world
But we in it shall be rememberèd;
We few, we happy few, we band of brothers –
For he today that sheds his blood with me
Shall be my brother; be he ne'er so vile,
This day shall gentle his condition.
And gentlemen in England now a-bed
Shall think themselves accurs'd they were not here,
And hold their manhoods cheap whiles any speaks
That fought with us upon Saint Crispin's day. 99

*(Act 4, scene 3, lines 20–57)*

GLOSSARY
*coz* – cousin (i.e. Westmoreland)
*crowns for convoy* – money for his journey home
*the feast of Crispian* – 25 October, the joint feast day for Saints Crispin
  and Crispian

# Henry VI, Part Three

WHO ☞ *Richard, Duke of Gloucester, later Richard III.*

WHERE ☞ *The Tower of London, c. 1460.*

WHO ELSE IS THERE ☞ *Richard is alone with the body of King Henry VI who he has just killed.*

WHAT IS HAPPENING ☞ *The hunchbacked Richard, Duke of Gloucester, has been scheming against the Lancastrian family, whose members have been the Kings Henry IV, V and VI, in order to claim the English throne. He has just killed King Henry and revels in his death. Only his brothers, Clarence and Edward, now stand between him and the crown.*

WHAT TO THINK ABOUT ☞

- *Richard has only just killed the King. He is not even certain that he is dead.*

- *He relishes his blood-thirsty act as he watches the blood drip from his sword: 'my sword weeps'.*

- *Think how fired up and breathless he must be from having just thrust his sword into the King and how much he enjoys stabbing the body again.*

- *There is humour in the way Richard recounts his own birth and mimics the voices of the women as they saw him being born. He is hunchbacked and club-footed which give opportunities for physical characterisation with the speech.*

WHERE ELSE TO LOOK ☞ *Other speeches revelling in villainy are from Aaron (Titus Andronicus, p. 92), Edmund (King Lear, p. 110) and Richard (Richard III, p. 78).*

### *Richard, Duke of Gloucester*

**66** What, will the aspiring blood of Lancaster*
Sink in the ground? I thought it would have mounted.
See how my sword weeps for the poor King's death.
O, may such purple tears be always shed
From those that wish the downfall of our house.

If any spark of life be yet remaining,
Down, down to hell, and say I sent thee thither.
(*Stabs the King again.*)
I, that have neither pity, love, nor fear.
Indeed 'tis true that Henry told me of;
For I have often heard my mother say,
I came into the world with my legs forward.*
Had I not reason, think ye, to make haste,
And seek their ruin that usurp'd our right?
The midwife wonder'd, and the women cried
'O, Jesus bless us, he is born with teeth!'
And so I was, which plainly signified,
That I should snarl, and bite and play the dog.
Then since the heavens have shaped my body so,
Let hell make crook'd my mind to answer it.
I have no brother, I am like no brother.
And this word 'love', which greybeards call divine,
Be resident in men like one another,
And not in me. I am myself alone.
Clarence, beware, thou keep'st me from the light,*
But I will sort a pitchy* day for thee;
For I will buzz abroad such prophecies
That Edward* shall be fearful of his life,
And then to purge his fear, I'll be thy death.
King Henry and the Prince his son* are gone;
Clarence, thy turn is next, and then the rest,
Counting myself but bad, till I be best.
I'll throw thy body in another room,
And triumph, Henry, in thy day of doom. **99**

(*Act 5, scene 6, lines 61–93*)

GLOSSARY

*Lancaster* – King Henry
*I came into the world with my legs forward* – was born the wrong way
    with his feet first.
*Clarence . . . keep'st me from the light* – his brother Clarence is in line to
    the throne before him
*pitchy* – pitch black          *Edward* – his other brother
*the Prince his son* – another Edward, Prince of Wales and son of King
    Henry

# Richard III

WHO ☞ *Richard, Duke of Gloucester, later Richard III.*

WHERE ☞ *A street in London, c. 1460.*

WHO ELSE IS THERE ☞ *Richard is alone.*

WHAT IS HAPPENING ☞ *Richard, Duke of Gloucester, has wooed Lady Anne whose husband he has killed, as she was mourning over the body of Henry VI, another of his victims.*

WHAT TO THINK ABOUT ☞

- *Richard is enjoying revelling in his villainy to the audience.*

- *The one word 'Ha' fills a whole line. Try and fill the line with the sound and the thoughts behind it.*

- *He is hunchbacked and club-footed which give opportunities for physical characterisation with the speech.*

- *Decide what Richard feels about his deformities and what he feels about women.*

WHERE ELSE TO LOOK ☞ *Other villains who make no apology for their actions are Aaron (Titus Andronicus, p. 92) and Edmund (King Lear, p. 110).*

## *Richard, Duke of Gloucester*

**❝** Was ever woman in this humour wooed?
Was ever woman in this humour won?
I'll have her – but I will not keep her long.
What, I that kill'd her husband and his father,
To take her in her heart's extremest hate,
With curses in her mouth, tears in her eyes,
The bleeding witness of my hatred by,
Having God, her conscience, and these bars* against me,
And I no friends to back my suit withal
But the plain devil and dissembling looks?

And yet to win her, all the world to nothing!*
Ha!
Hath she forgot already that brave prince,
Edward,* her lord, whom I, some three months since,
Stabb'd in my angry mood at Tewkesbury?*
A sweeter and a lovelier gentleman,
Fram'd in the prodigality of nature,
Young, valiant, wise, and, no doubt, right royal,
The spacious world cannot again afford.
And will she yet debase her eyes on me,
That cropp'd the golden prime of this sweet prince,
And made her widow to a woeful bed?
On me, whose all not equals Edward's moiety?*
On me, that halt* and am misshapen thus?
Upon my life, she finds – although I cannot -
Myself to be a marvellous proper man.
I'll be at charges for* a looking-glass,
And entertain some score or two of tailors
To study fashions to adorn my body.
But first I'll turn yon fellow* in his grave,
And then return lamenting to my love.
Shine out, fair sun, till I have bought a glass,*
That I may see my shadow as I pass. 〝

(*Act 1, scene 2, lines 227–63, with some cuts*)


GLOSSARY
*bars* – impediments
*all the world to nothing* – in trying to win Lady Anne, Richard's chances
    are all the world against nothing
*Edward* – the Prince of Wales, son of Henry VI, whom Richard has
    killed
*Tewkesbury* – battle where Richard killed Edward
*moiety* – half
*halt* – limp (because of his club foot)
*I'll be at charges for* – I'll order
*yon fellow* – the corpse of King Henry VI
*glass* – mirror

# Richard III

WHO ☞    *Henry, Duke of Richmond.*

WHERE ☞    *Bosworth Field, two miles outside the town of Bosworth in Leicestershire, August 1485.*

WHO ELSE IS THERE ☞    *Richmond's army.*

WHAT IS HAPPENING ☞    *About to confront King Richard at the battle of Bosworth, Henry, Duke of Richmond, rallies his troops. After his victory in this battle, during which King Richard is slain, he will become King Henry VII.*

WHAT TO THINK ABOUT ☞

- *Richmond is firing up his troops for battle.*
- *He tells them that they have right on their side.*
- *He talks of God.*
- *He describes their enemy as a 'bloody tyrant'.*
- *The language and metre is very controlled and measured.*
- *Use the five-times repeated device of 'If…' as a series of stepping stones, possibly increasing and decreasing volume, speed, direction etc.*
- *The ending with its rhyming couplet and use of the word 'cheerfully' is very upbeat and positive.*

WHERE ELSE TO LOOK ☞    *Also rallying their troops are the Constable of France (Henry V, p. 72), Henry (Henry V, p. 74) and Richmond's adversary Richard (Richard III, p. 82).*

## Henry, Duke of Richmond

**❝** More than I have said, loving countrymen,
The leisure and enforcement of the time
Forbids to dwell upon. Yet remember this:
God, and our good cause, fight upon our side.
The prayers of holy saints and wrongèd souls,
Like high-rear'd bulwarks stand before our faces;

Richard except,* those whom we fight against
Had rather have us win than him they follow.
For what is he they follow? Truly, gentlemen,
A bloody tyrant and a homicide;
One rais'd in blood, and one in blood establish'd;
One that made means to come by what he hath,
And slaughter'd those that were the means to help him;
A base, foul stone, made precious by the foil*
Of England's chair,* where he is falsely set;
One that hath ever been God's enemy.
Then, if you fight against God's enemy,
God will in justice ward* you as His soldiers;
If you do sweat to put a tyrant down,
You sleep in peace, the tyrant being slain;
If you do fight against your country's foes,
Your country's fat shall pay your pains the hire;
If you do fight in safeguard of your wives,
Your wives shall welcome home the conquerors;
If you do free your children from the sword,
Your children's children quits* it in your age.
Then, in the name of God and all these rights,
Advance your standards, draw your willing swords.
For me, the ransom* of my bold attempt
Shall be this cold corpse on the earth's cold face;
But if I thrive, the gain of my attempt
The least of you shall share his part thereof.
Sound drums and trumpets boldly and cheerfully,
God and Saint George! Richmond and victory! 🙶

(*Act 5 scene 3, lines 239–72*)

GLOSSARY

*Richard except* – with the exception of Richard
*foil* – golden setting
*England's chair* – the throne
*ward* – reward
*quits it* – repays you
*ransom* – penalty for failure

# Richard III

WHO ☞ *King Richard.*

WHERE ☞ *Bosworth Field, two miles outside the town of Bosworth in Leicestershire, August 1485.*

WHO ELSE IS THERE ☞ *Richard's army.*

WHAT IS HAPPENING ☞ *Before the Battle of Bosworth Richard rallies his troops, despite having been unnerved by nightmares the night before.*

WHAT TO THINK ABOUT ☞

- *Richard exhorts his troops by his descriptions of their enemy.*

- *It is the enemy's weaknesses not his army's strengths that he talks about.*

- *There is chauvinism in his talk of the Breton soldiers they are about to fight.*

- *He breaks into a strong rhythm in the final lines as the battle is about to begin with the word 'boldly' being given strength by its adding to the length of the line.*

WHERE ELSE TO LOOK ☞ *Also rallying his troops is Richard's adversary Richmond (Richard III, p. 80) as are the Constable of France (Henry V, p. 72) and Henry (Henry V, p. 74).*

## King Richard

**❝** What shall I say more than I have inferr'd?
Remember whom you are to cope* withal;
A sort of vagabonds, rascals, and runaways;
A scum of Bretons * and base lackey-peasants
Whom their o'er-cloyèd* country vomits forth
To desperate adventures and assur'd destruction.
You sleeping safe, they bring to you unrest;

You having lands, and bless'd with beauteous wives,
They would restrain* the one, distain* the other.
And who doth lead them but a paltry fellow,
Long kept in Bretagne* at our mother's cost?
A milksop!* One that never in his life
Felt so much cold as over-shoes in snow!
Let's whip these stragglers o'er the seas again;
Lash hence these overweening rags of France,
These famish'd beggars, weary of their lives,
Who, but for dreaming on this fond exploit,
For want of means – poor rats – had hang'd themselves.
If we be conquer'd, let men conquer us,
And not these bastard Bretons whom our fathers
Have in their own land beaten, bobb'd, and thump'd,
And in record, left them the heirs of shame.
Shall these enjoy our lands? Lie with our wives?
Ravish our daughters?

*Drum afar off.*

Hark! I hear their drum!
Fight, gentlemen of England, fight, boldly, yeomen!
Draw, archers, draw your arrows to the head!
Spur your proud horses hard, and ride in blood!
Amaze the welkin* with your broken staves!* 🙶

(*Act 5, scene 3, lines 315–42*)


GLOSSARY

*cope* – encounter, grapple with
*a scum of Bretons* – Richmond's army includes French forces brought
    with him from Brittany
*o'er-cloyèd* – over-stuffed, engorged
*restrain* – withhold from you
*distain* – defile, rape
*Bretagne* – Brittany
*milksop* – feeble man
*welkin* – sky, heavens
*broken staves* – staffs broken on the heads of the enemy

# Henry VIII

WHO ☞    *Cardinal Wolsey, the senior, most influential churchman in England at the time.*

WHERE ☞    *A room in the Palace of Westminster, c. 1530.*

WHO ELSE IS THERE ☞    *Wolsey is alone.*

WHAT IS HAPPENING ☞    *The Duke of Norfolk has just read out a long list of charges against Wolsey and asked for the return of his seal of office. His downfall having been made clear to him, Wolsey reflects on his state.*

WHAT TO THINK ABOUT ☞

• *Wolsey is alone with his thoughts.*

• *His career is at an end and he accepts this with resignation.*

• *There is a break in the middle of the speech after the word 'depth'. The pause gives Wolsey's thoughts time to move to contemplation of his own pride.*

• *He equates himself with Lucifer, the great angel who fell from heaven to become Satan.*

• *Decide how Wolsey feels and how to play the combination of ruefulness, bitterness, resentment, pride, hurt and acceptance in the speech.*

WHERE ELSE TO LOOK ☞    *Powerful men left alone to reflect on their situations are Henry (Henry IV, Part Two, p. 66), Macbeth (Macbeth, pp. 102 and 104) and Claudius (Hamlet, p. 106).*

## *Wolsey*

**"** So, farewell to the little good you* bear me.
Farewell? A long farewell, to all my greatness.
This is the state of man. Today he puts forth
The tender leaves of hopes, tomorrow blossoms,
And bears his blushing honours thick upon him.
The third day comes a frost, a killing frost,
And, when he thinks, good easy man, full surely
His greatness is a-ripening, nips his root,
And then he falls as I do. I have ventured
Like little wanton boys that swim on bladders,*
This many summers in a sea of glory,
But far beyond my depth. My high-blown pride
At length broke under me, and now has left me,
Weary and old with service, to the mercy
Of a rude stream that must for ever hide me.
Vain pomp and glory of this world, I hate ye.
I feel my heart new open'd. O how wretched
Is that poor man that hangs on princes' favours!
There is betwixt that smile we would aspire to,
That sweet aspect of princes, and their ruin,
More pangs and fears than wars or women have;
And when he falls, he falls like Lucifer,
Never to hope again. **"**

(*Act 3, scene 2, lines 351–73*)

GLOSSARY

*you* – the Duke of Norfolk
*bladders* – inflated bags, water-wings

# The Tragedies

# Troilus and Cressida

WHO ☞  *Troilus, a young Trojan.*

WHERE ☞  *Ilium, the palace of King Priam of Troy, during the war between the Ancient Greeks and the Trojans.*

WHO ELSE IS THERE ☞  *Pandarus, Cressida's uncle.*

WHAT IS HAPPENING ☞  *Troilus confesses to Pandarus how much he is in love with his niece Cressida and complains that Pandarus's praise of Cressida only increases the pain of his so far unrequited love.*

WHAT TO THINK ABOUT ☞

- *Troilus pictures himself as wounded by love and complains that everything Pandarus says about Cressida only makes his wounds more painful.*

- *Decide how much Troilus is genuinely pained and how much he is putting it on for effect.*

- *Pandarus is the person through whom Troilus can get to Cressida and so it is vital that he convinces him of the strength of his love.*

- *The speech ends with a very short, very dramatic line that can be played for all it is worth.*

WHERE ELSE TO LOOK ☞  *Other young men head-over-heels in love in their different ways are Berowne (Love's Labour's Lost, p. 38) and Proteus (The Two Gentlemen of Verona, p. 22).*

## *Troilus*

**❝** O Pandarus! I tell thee, Pandarus –
When I do tell thee there my hopes lie drown'd,
Reply not in how many fathoms deep
They lie indrench'd.* I tell thee I am mad
In Cressid's love: thou answer'st 'She is fair',
Pour'st in the open ulcer of my heart
Her eyes, her hair, her cheek, her gait, her voice;
Handlest in thy discourse,* O, that her hand,
In whose comparison all whites are ink,*
Writing their own reproach, to whose soft seizure
The cygnet's down* is harsh and spirit of sense
Hard as the palm of ploughman: this thou tell'st me,
As true thou tell'st me, when I say I love her;
But, saying thus, instead of oil and balm,*
Thou lay'st in every gash that love hath given me
The knife that made it. **❞**

*(Act 1, scene 1, lines 49–64)*

GLOSSARY

*indrench'd* – drowned
*handlest in thy discourse* – assert in your disquisition
*her hand, / In whose comparison all whites are ink* – her hand is so pale
   that all colours of white are black as ink in comparison
*cygnet's down* – the feathers of a young swan that are not as soft as
   Cressida's touch (her 'soft seizure')
*balm* – soothing medicine

# Titus Andronicus

WHO ☞    *Titus, a Roman general.*

WHERE ☞    *A street in Ancient Rome.*

WHO ELSE IS THERE ☞    *Titus's brother Marcus, his sons Martius, Lucius and Quintus and his daughter Lavinia.*

WHAT IS HAPPENING ☞    *After victory in battle Titus allows the ritual sacrifice of the son of Tamora, the defeated Queen of the Goths. She and her other sons get their revenge through the mutilation of Titus's daughter Lavinia. Titus has just found her raped, her hands cut off and her tongue torn out. He is desperate to know who has done this to her.*

WHAT TO THINK ABOUT ☞

- *Titus is suffering almost unimaginable anguish.*

- *He could be crying out loudly in his suffering; or he could be quiet and in a state of shock. It is possible to play between and including these two extremes.*

- *His hands are physically important in the speech with his references to self-harm. Decide how he might he use them during the speech.*

WHERE ELSE TO LOOK ☞    *Pericles (Pericles, p. 54) is also suffering great anguish.*

## *Titus*

**❝** Speak, Lavinia, what accursèd hand
Hath made thee handless in thy father's sight?
What fool hath added water to the sea,
Or brought a faggot to bright-burning Troy?
My grief was at the height before thou cam'st,
And now like Nilus* it disdaineth bounds.
Give me a sword, I'll chop off my hands too,
For they have fought for Rome, and all in vain.
And they have nursed this woe, in feeding life;*
In bootless prayer have they been held up,
And they have served me to effectless use.
Now all the service I require of them
Is that the one will help to cut the other.
'Tis well, Lavinia, that thou hast no hands,
For hands to do Rome service is but vain. **❞**

*(Act 3, scene 1, lines 64–78)*

GLOSSARY

*Nilus* – the river Nile, famous for its seasonal floods
*they have nursed this woe, in feeding life* – by nourishing her life, Titus's
 hands have merely prepared his daughter for this misery

# Titus Andronicus

WHO ☞    *Aaron, a villainous Moor.*

WHERE ☞    *The plains outside Ancient Rome.*

WHO ELSE IS THERE ☞    *Lucius, son of his enemy Titus Andronicus, an army of Goths and Aaron's new child, born of his secret liaison with the Queen of the Goths.*

WHAT IS HAPPENING ☞    *Captured by his enemies and about to be hanged, the villainous Aaron is asked if he is 'not sorry for these heinous deeds'. Aaron replies that he revels in his villainy and that his only regret is that he has not carried out even more hideous acts.*

WHAT TO THINK ABOUT ☞

- *Aaron is enjoying himself. He is being shocking and loves to shock.*

- *Each of the actions he talks about is a separate story, from ravishing a maid to setting fire to haystacks, all contained in one sentence ten lines long.*

- *He wants to get a reaction and comes up with one story after another to achieve this. Allow time for those reactions.*

- *The words and stories are themselves so shocking they may need little vocal embellishment.*

- *The story of digging up the dead might be told quietly and scarily.*

WHERE ELSE TO LOOK ☞    *Richard (Henry VI, Part Three, p. 76) and Edmund (King Lear, p. 110) both also revel in their nastiness.*

### *Aaron*

**"** Even now I curse the day – and yet I think
Few come within the compass of my curse –
Wherein I did not some notorious ill,
As kill a man, or else devise his death,
Ravish a maid, or plot the way to do it,
Accuse some innocent, and forswear myself,
Set deadly enmity between two friends,
Make poor men's cattle break their necks,
Set fire on barns and hay-stacks in the night,
And bid the owners quench them with their tears.
Oft have I digg'd up dead men from their graves,
And set them upright at their dear friends' doors,
Even when their sorrows almost were forgot,
And on their skins, as on the bark of trees,
Have with my knife carvèd in Roman letters,
'Let not your sorrow die, though I am dead.'
Tut, I have done a thousand dreadful things
As willingly as one would kill a fly,
And nothing grieves me heartily indeed
But that I cannot do ten thousand more. **"**

*(Act 5, scene 1, lines 125–44)*

# Romeo and Juliet

WHO ☞ *Prince Escalus, ruler of Verona.*

WHERE ☞ *A public place in Verona, Italy.*

WHO ELSE IS THERE ☞ *Members of the well-to-do rival Capulet and Montague families and others.*

WHAT IS HAPPENING ☞ *The Montagues and Capulets are fighting once again and the Prince comes in to halt the brawls that are disturbing his city of Verona.*

WHAT TO THINK ABOUT ☞

- *There is storytelling happening here as the Prince sets out for the audience the background to the events they are watching.*

- *Plan the geography of the scene – which families and which individuals are where.*

- *The Prince is expressing his anger at the families involved in the dispute but also speaking to a wider public.*

- *It takes a while for him to be heard above the clamour.*

- *Allow time for the Prince to take control of the situation.*

- *Make sure that his final order is likely to be obeyed.*

WHERE ELSE TO LOOK ☞ *Public anger of a different sort is expressed by the Duke of York (Richard II, p. 60).*

## *Prince Escalus*

**"** Rebellious subjects, enemies to peace,
Profaners of this neighbour-stainèd steel,\*
Will they not hear? What ho, you men, you beasts,
That quench the fire of your pernicious rage,
With purple fountains issuing from your veins:
On pain of torture, from those bloody hands
Throw your mistemper'd weapons to the ground,
And hear the sentence of your movèd Prince.
Three civil brawls, bred of an airy word,
By thee old Capulet and Montague,
Have thrice disturb'd the quiet of our streets,
And made Verona's ancient citizens
Cast by\* their grave-beseeming ornaments\*
To wield old partisans,\* in hands as old,
Canker'd\* with peace, to part your canker'd hate.\*
If ever you disturb our streets again,
Your lives shall pay the forfeit of the peace.
For this time, all the rest depart away.
You, Capulet, shall go along with me,
And Montague, come you this afternoon,
To know our further pleasure in this case,
To old Freetown,\* our common judgment-place.
Once more, on pain of death, all men depart. **"**

(*Act 1, scene 1, lines 78–100*)

GLOSSARY

*neighbour-stainèd steel* – swords stained with neighbours' blood
*cast by* – throw off
*grave-beseeming ornaments* – suitably austere garments
*partisans* – large sword-like weapons
*canker'd* – decayed
*canker'd hate* – malignant hate (Shakespeare uses the word 'canker'd'
    with two different meanings)
*Freetown* – location of the city's courtroom

# Timon of Athens

WHO ☞ *Alcibiades, an Athenian captain.*

WHERE ☞ *Outside the gates of Athens in Ancient Greece.*

WHO ELSE IS THERE ☞ *Alcibiades is alone.*

WHAT IS HAPPENING ☞ *As a soldier, Alcibiades has risked his life to protect Athens. He has asked the Athenian Senate to pardon a friend condemned to death for murder. The Senators have refused and after Alcibiades questions their authority he is banished and left to rue his fate.*

WHAT TO THINK ABOUT ☞

- *Alcibiades' opening two lines are directed at the Senators who have banished him, asking that the gods decay them to ugly skeletons.*

- *He starts cursing the Senators and ends with a plan. Chart that journey.*

- *He is as angry with himself as he is with the Athenians who have banished him.*

- *The single word 'Banishment' in the middle of the speech is full of performance possibilities.*

- *Alcibiades turns things around in his mind and makes his banishment a positive.*

- *He remembers his troops and that thought is key to his plan for revenge.*

WHERE ELSE TO LOOK ☞ *The Duke of York (Richard II, p. 60) rebukes an authority more powerful than himself, and Shylock (The Merchant of Venice, p. 44) also rails against his enemies.*

## *Alcibiades*

**❝** Now the gods keep you old enough, that you may live
Only in bone, that none may look on you.
I'm worse than mad. I have kept back their foes
While they have told* their money, and let out
Their coin upon large interest; I myself
Rich only in large hurts. All those, for this?
Is this the balsam* that the usuring senate
Pours into captains' wounds? Banishment!
It comes not ill. I hate not to be banish'd,
It is a cause worthy my spleen and fury,
That I may strike at Athens. I'll cheer up
My discontented troops, and lay for hearts.*
'Tis honour with most lands to be at odds,
Soldiers should brook* as little wrongs as gods. **❞**

(*Act 3, scene 5, lines 106–19*)

GLOSSARY

*told* – counted
*balsam* – healing ointment
*lay for hearts* – arrange to win their support
*brook* – put up with

# Julius Caesar

WHO ☞ *Brutus, conspirator against Caesar.*

WHERE ☞ *Brutus's orchard in Ancient Rome, c. 44 BC.*

WHO ELSE IS THERE ☞ *Brutus is alone.*

WHAT IS HAPPENING ☞ *Julius Caesar appears ambitious to be crowned emperor and so become sole ruler of Rome. Talking to himself, Brutus debates his conflicting duties between his love and respect for Caesar and his patriotism for Rome. He convinces himself that Caesar must be killed for the greater good.*

WHAT TO THINK ABOUT ☞

- *This is a very measured speech, carefully argued. Decide how much of this Brutus has worked out already.*

- *Perhaps he is going over things one last time to be sure or perhaps he still has to convince himself.*

- *Work through his arguments carefully as the personal conflicts with the political in his heart, mind and soul. Brutus can think of nothing in Caesar's nature to despise but fears his nature will be changed by being crowned emperor.*

- *He argues that nobility is corrupted when it separates itself from the power it wields, though he has not known that yet to happen with Caesar.*

- *As there is nothing intrinsically dangerous in Caesar, Brutus has to think of him as a serpent's egg that has danger within it.*

WHERE ELSE TO LOOK ☞ *Macbeth (Macbeth, p. 104) is also contemplating the necessity of murder.*

## *Brutus*

**❝** It must be by his death; and, for my part,
I know no personal cause to spurn at* him,
But for the general.* He would be crown'd:
How that might change his nature, there's the question.
It is the bright day that brings forth the adder,*
And that craves wary walking. Crown him that,
And then I grant we put a sting in him
That at his will he may do danger with.*
Th'abuse of greatness is when it disjoins
Remorse from power, and, to speak truth of Caesar,
I have not known when his affections sway'd
More than his reason. But 'tis a common proof
That lowliness is young ambition's ladder,
Whereto the climber upward turns his face;
But when he once attains the upmost round,*
He then unto the ladder turns his back,
Looks in the clouds, scorning the base degrees
By which he did ascend: so Caesar may.
Then, lest he may, prevent!* And since the quarrel
Will bear no colour* for the thing he is,
Fashion it thus: that what he is, augmented,
Would run to these and these extremities;
And therefore think him as a serpent's egg
Which, hatch'd, would, as his kind grow mischievous,
And kill him in the shell. **❞**

*(Act 2, scene 1, lines 10–34)*

GLOSSARY

*spurn at* – despise
*for the general* – Brutus only has a general cause (in the name of a
    collective benefit) to despise Caesar, not a specific personal one
*the bright day that brings forth the adder* – snakes come out when the sun
    shines
*we put a sting in him / That at his will he may do danger with* – if we
    crown him we give him a weapon that he can cause trouble with
*round* – rung
*lest he may, prevent* – in case he does we must stop him
*colour* – mitigating excuse

# Julius Caesar

WHO ☞    *Mark Antony.*

WHERE ☞    *Ancient Rome, in front of the Capitol, 15 March 44 BC.*

WHO ELSE IS THERE ☞    *The body of Julius Caesar, with Brutus, Cassius, Casca and the others who have assassinated him. There is also a large crowd.*

WHAT IS HAPPENING ☞    *Caesar has just been assassinated and the conspirators have washed their hands in his blood and declared their devotion to political liberty. Antony comes to meet with the conspirators and discuss joining them. He tells the conspirators that if they plan to kill him too, to do it now.*

WHAT TO THINK ABOUT ☞

- *Antony begins by talking to the body of Caesar, whom he has admired.*

- *The situation for Antony is very dangerous and he fears, as a friend of Caesar, that the conspirators may kill him next.*

- *Plot the geography of the scene and decide where Caesar's body is and where the assassins are that he is addressing.*

- *He talks of 'conquests, glories, triumphs, spoils'. Decide why he chooses these words and what resonance they have for him.*

WHERE ELSE TO LOOK ☞    *The Duke of York (Richard II, p. 60) also mixes grief and politics.*

## *Mark Antony*

**"** O mighty Caesar! Dost thou lie so low?
Are all thy conquests, glories, triumphs, spoils,
Shrunk to this little measure? Fare thee well.
I know not, gentlemen, what you intend,
Who else must be let blood, who else is rank.*
If I myself, there is no hour so fit
As Caesar's death's hour, nor no instrument
Of half that worth as those your swords, made rich
With the most noble blood of all this world.
I do beseech ye, if you bear me hard,*
Now, whilst your purpled* hands do reek and smoke,
Fulfil your pleasure. Live a thousand years,
I shall not find myself so apt to die:
No place will please me so, no mean of death,
As here by Caesar, and by you cut off,
The choice and master spirits of this age. **"**

*(Act 3, scene 1, lines 149–64)*

GLOSSARY

*rank* – diseased (and in need of blood-letting)
*bear me hard* – think ill of me
*purpled* – made dark red with blood

# Macbeth

WHO ☞    *Macbeth, a general in King Duncan's army.*

WHERE ☞    *A room in Macbeth's castle at Inverness, Scotland, historically the mid-11th century.*

WHO ELSE IS THERE ☞    *Macbeth is alone.*

WHAT IS HAPPENING ☞    *Witches have prophesied that Macbeth will become King of Scotland. In league with his wife he is on his way to kill King Duncan, who is a guest in his castle, and so attain his crown. As he goes to Duncan's room, Macbeth sees an imaginary dagger.*

WHAT TO THINK ABOUT ☞

- *Picture the dagger: what it looks like, where it is and whether and how it moves.*

- *Decide whether, when it reappears, the dagger is in the same place.*

- *Macbeth doubts his own sanity and wonders if the dagger is a vision of his troubled mind.*

- *His mood changes when he hears the bell and he springs into action. Decide how his resolution shows itself physically and vocally.*

WHERE ELSE TO LOOK ☞    *Alone at night with their thoughts are Henry (Henry IV, Part Two, p. 66), Claudius (Hamlet, p. 106) and Othello (Othello, p. 116).*

### Macbeth

**❝** Is this a dagger which I see before me,
The handle toward my hand? Come, let me clutch thee!
I have thee not, and yet I see thee still.
Art thou not, fatal vision, sensible
To feeling as to sight? Or art thou but

A dagger of the mind, a false creation
Proceeding from the heat-oppressèd* brain?
I see thee yet, in form as palpable
As this which now I draw.
Thou marshall'st* me the way that I was going,
And such an instrument I was to use.
Mine eyes are made the fools o' th'other senses,
Or else worth all the rest. I see thee still,
And on thy blade and dudgeon* gouts of blood,
Which was not so before. There's no such thing.
It is the bloody business which informs*
Thus to mine eyes. Now o'er the one half-world*
Nature seems dead, and wicked dreams abuse
The curtain'd sleep. Thou sure and firm-set earth,
Hear not my steps, which way they walk, for fear
Thy very stones prate* of my whereabout,
And take the present horror from the time,
Which now suits with it. Whiles I threat,* he lives:
Words to the heat of deeds too cold breath gives.

*A bell rings.*

I go, and it is done. The bell invites me.
Hear it not, Duncan, for it is a knell*
That summons thee to heaven or to hell. **99**

(*Act 2, scene 1, lines 33–64, with some cuts*)

GLOSSARY

*heat-oppressèd* – burdened or troubled with emotion
*marshall'st* – led
*dudgeon* – handle
*informs* – takes form
*the one half-world* – that half of the globe over which it is night
*Hecate* – the goddess of witchcraft
*prate* – talk
*threat* – threaten (but do nothing)
*knell* – bell that tolls at funerals

# Macbeth

WHO ☞ *Macbeth, King of Scotland.*

WHERE ☞ *A room in Macbeth's castle at Inverness, Scotland, historically the mid-11th century.*

WHO ELSE IS THERE ☞ *Macbeth is alone.*

WHAT IS HAPPENING ☞ *Macbeth and his friend Banquo met witches who prophesised that Macbeth would become King of Scotland and that Banquo's sons would become kings. Macbeth has murdered his way to the crown but does not feel his position to be safe until his friend Banquo is also killed.*

WHAT TO THINK ABOUT ☞

- *Macbeth has not thought through the consequences of killing the King and he is now haunted with paranoia and doubts.*

- *He is fearful of the witches' prophesies about Banquo's heirs.*

- *Macbeth remembers the encounter with the witches. Picture that scene.*

- *He moves on at the end of the speech and is full of resolution. Play that change.*

- *'Who's there?', at the very end, provides a sudden gear change showing Macbeth to be startled and anxious.*

WHERE ELSE TO LOOK ☞ *Othello (Othello, p. 116) is also contemplating murder as is Macbeth himself earlier in the play (Macbeth, p. 102). Alone at night with their thoughts are Henry (Henry IV, Part Two, p. 66) and Claudius (Hamlet, p. 106).*

## Macbeth

**❝** To be thus is nothing,
But to be safely thus. Our fears in Banquo
Stick deep, and in his royalty of nature*
Reigns that which would be fear'd. 'Tis much he dares,

And, to that dauntless temper of his mind
He hath a wisdom that doth guide his valour
To act in safety. There is none but he
Whose being I do fear, and under him,
My genius* is rebuk'd, as it is said,
Mark Antony's was by Caesar.* He chid* the sisters
When first they put the name of king upon me,
And bade them speak to him; then prophet-like
They hail'd him father to a line of kings.
Upon my head they placed a fruitless crown,
And put a barren sceptre in my grip,
Thence to be wrench'd with an unlineal* hand,
No son of mine succeeding. If 't be so,
For Banquo's issue* have I fil'd* my mind,
For them the gracious Duncan have I murder'd,
Put rancours* in the vessel of my peace
Only for them, and mine eternal jewel*
Given to the common enemy of man*
To make them kings, the seed of Banquo kings.
Rather than so, come, Fate, into the list*
And champion me to the utterance!* Who's there? 99

*(Act 3, scene 1, lines 47–71)*

GLOSSARY

*royalty of nature* – natural regality, noble bearing
*genius* – soul
*my genius is rebuked as . . . Mark Antony's was by Caesar* – Octavius
    Caesar was said to overpower Mark Antony's spirit
*chid* – told off, argued with
*unlineal* – of a different family
*issue* – children
*fil'd* – defiled
*rancours* – hatred
*eternal jewel* – soul
*the common enemy of man* – Satan, the Devil
*list* – fighting arena at a tournament
*utterance* – utmost, last extremity, death

# Hamlet

WHO ☞    *Claudius, King of Denmark.*

WHERE ☞    *A room in the royal castle of Elsinore, Denmark.*

WHO ELSE IS THERE ☞    *Claudius is alone.*

WHAT IS HAPPENING ☞    *Claudius has killed his own brother, married his brother's wife and become King of Denmark. Contemplating the guilt of his actions, Claudius attempts to pray.*

WHAT TO THINK ABOUT ☞

- *Claudius is thinking back on the sins he has committed.*

- *He focuses on his murder of his own brother – the primal eldest curse (i.e. the first crime in the Bible when Cain killed his brother Abel).*

- *Decide how much he really wants to pray and how much he wants forgiveness.*

- *He thinks of the things, the effects, he still possesses as a result of the murder of his brother.*

- *Claudius has much to think about and is in no rush. Allow the thoughts time to come one from the other.*

WHERE ELSE TO LOOK ☞    *Macbeth (Macbeth, pp. 102 and 104) and Henry (Henry IV, Part Two, p. 66) are other kings alone with their thoughts.*

### Claudius

❝ Oh, my offence is rank,\* it smells to heaven.
It hath the primal eldest curse upon't:
A brother's murder. Pray can I not.
Though inclination be as sharp as will,
My stronger guilt defeats my strong intent,
And, like a man to double business bound,
I stand in pause where I shall first begin,
And both neglect. What if this cursèd hand
Were thicker than itself with brother's blood?

Is there not rain enough in the sweet heavens
To wash it white as snow? Whereto serves mercy
But to confront the visage* of offence?
And what's in prayer but this two-fold force:
To be forestallèd ere we come to fall,
Or pardon'd being down? Then I'll look up.
My fault is past – but oh, what form of prayer
Can serve my turn? 'Forgive me my foul murder'?
That cannot be, since I am still possess'd
Of those effects for which I did the murder:
My crown, mine own ambition, and my queen.
May one be pardon'd and retain the offence?
In the corrupted currents of this world
Offence's gilded hand may shove by justice;*
And oft 'tis seen the wicked prize itself
Buys out the law. But 'tis not so above.
There is no shuffling;* there the action lies
In his true nature, and we ourselves compell'd,
Even to the teeth and forehead of our faults,*
To give in evidence. What then? What rests?
Try what repentance can. What can it not?
Yet what can it when one cannot repent?
O wretched state! O bosom black as death!
O limèd* soul, that, struggling to be free
Art more engag'd! Help, angels! Make assay.*
Bow, stubborn knees, and, heart with strings of steel,
Be soft as sinews of the newborn babe.
All may be well. 🙶

(*Act 3, scene 3, lines 36–72*)

GLOSSARY

*rank* – foul, serious, gross          *visage* – appearance
*offence's gilded hand may shove by justice* – a rich criminal can evade
    justice
*shuffling* – deceit, trickery
*even to the teeth and forehead of our faults* – to the utmost of our sins
*limèd* – like a snared bird
*make assay* – try

# Hamlet

WHO ☞ *Hamlet, Prince of Denmark.*

WHERE ☞ *The royal castle of Elsinore, Denmark.*

WHO ELSE IS THERE ☞ *King Claudius is kneeling in the next room appearing to pray.*

WHAT IS HAPPENING ☞ *Claudius has become King by murdering Hamlet's father and marrying Hamlet's mother. Coming across the King, Hamlet sees an opportunity to kill him in revenge for the murder of his own father but then thinks that as he is at prayer Claudius will therefore go straight to heaven if he is killed.*

WHAT TO THINK ABOUT ☞

- *Hamlet has been waiting for an opportunity to take his revenge on Claudius throughout the play. Now he has the chance but stops himself. Decide how close he comes to killing the King before he hesitates.*

- *The word 'No' fills a line, giving him time to think what to say and do next.*

- *Find images for all the sinful acts that Hamlet knows Claudius to have committed so that each is real to him.*

- *Hamlet is on his way to see his mother when he discovers Claudius and he remembers her at the end of the speech.*

WHERE ELSE TO LOOK ☞ *Richard, Duke of Gloucester (Henry VI, Part Three, p. 76), Macbeth (Macbeth, pp. 102 and 104) and Othello (Othello, p. 116) all have very different thoughts about killing.*

## *Hamlet*

**❝** Now might I do it pat,* now he is praying.
And now I'll do't. – And so he goes to heaven,
And so am I reveng'd. That would be scann'd.*
A villain kills my father, and for that,
I, his sole son, do this same villain send
To heaven.
O, this is hire and salary, not revenge.
He took my father grossly,* full of bread,
With all his crimes broad blown,* as fresh as May,
And how his audit stands, who knows save heaven?*
But in our circumstance and course of thought,
'Tis heavy with him. And am I then reveng'd,
To take him in the purging of his soul,
When he is fit and season'd for his passage?*
No.
Up, sword, and know thou a more horrid hent:*
When he is drunk asleep, or in his rage,
Or in th'incestuous pleasure of his bed,
At gaming, swearing, or about some act
That has no relish of salvation in't –
Then trip him, that his heels may kick at heaven,
And that his soul may be as damn'd and black
As hell, whereto it goes. My mother stays.*
This physic* but prolongs thy sickly days. **❞**

(*Act 3, scene 3, lines 73–96*)

GLOSSARY

*pat* – opportunely
*scann'd* – criticised
*grossly* – with his sins unabsolved
*broad blown* – in full bloom
*how his audit stands, who knows save heaven* – only heaven knows the
    state of Claudius' soul
*season'd for his passage* – ready to meet his maker
*hent* – opportunity
*stays* – waits
*physic* – medicine

# King Lear

WHO ☞  *Edmund, illegitimate son of the Earl of Gloucester.*

WHERE ☞  *A room in the Earl of Gloucester's castle in ancient Britain.*

WHO ELSE IS THERE ☞  *Edmund is alone.*

WHAT IS HAPPENING ☞  *His father, the Earl of Gloucester, has just blamed the forces of astrology for man's fate and bad behaviour. Alone, Edmund says this is just an evasion of the truth and revels in his own wickedness.*

WHAT TO THINK ABOUT ☞

- *The speech can be played introspectively or out to the audience.*

- *Edmund is unapologetic for his behaviour and blames no one but himself.*

- *The fact that he is a bastard is crucial to his self-image and it ends the speech.*

- *Consider which of the types he mentions is true of himself: knaves, thieves, treachers, drunkards, liars and adulterers.*

- *Some of these types might be in the audience in front of him.*

- *Relish how distasteful the word 'compounded' can be when used to describe one's parents having sex.*

WHERE ELSE TO LOOK ☞  *Aaron (Titus Andronicus, p. 92) and Richard (Richard III, p. 78) both also revel in their nastiness.*

## Edmund

**"** This is the excellent foppery* of the world, that when
we are sick in fortune, often the surfeit* of our own
behaviour, we make guilty of our disasters the sun, the
moon, and stars – as if we were villains on necessity; fools by
heavenly compulsion; knaves, thieves, and treachers* by
spherical predominance;* drunkards, liars, and adulterers by
an enforced obedience of planetary influence; and all that we
are evil in by a divine thrusting on! An admirable evasion of
whoremaster* man, to lay his goatish* disposition on the
charge of a star! 'My father compounded* with my mother
under the Dragon's tail,* and my nativity was under *Ursa
Major*,* so that it follows I am rough and lecherous.' I should
have been that I am, had the maidenliest* star in the
firmament twinkled on my bastardising. **"**

(*Act 1, scene 2, lines 116 onwards*)

GLOSSARY

*foppery* – foolishness
*surfeit* – sickness through over-indulgence
*treachers* – cheats, traitors
*spherical predominance* – ascendancy of the stars
*whoremaster* – lecherous (literally someone who goes with prostitutes)
*goatish* – lecherous
*compounded* – had sex with
*Dragon's tail* – point between orbits of moon and sun
*Ursa Major* – constellation of the Great Bear
*maidenliest* – most virginal

# King Lear

WHO ☞    *Edgar, banished son of the Earl of Gloucester.*

WHERE ☞    *The open countryside in ancient Britain.*

WHO ELSE IS THERE ☞    *Edgar is alone.*

WHAT IS HAPPENING ☞    *In order to escape capture by his father, who wrongly believes Edgar to be plotting against him, Edgar disguises himself as 'Poor Tom', a mad beggar.*

WHAT TO THINK ABOUT ☞

• *The opening line is short, perhaps because Edgar is out of breath.*

• *Edgar starts the scene as himself, evading capture, and ends it in the disguised character of Poor Tom. Work out how to make that physical and vocal change.*

• *Decide where the urgency to 'preserve' himself comes from.*

• *Decide where the idea of Poor Tom comes from and whether it is a sudden thought or a gradual process.*

• *Think how safe or how vulnerable Edgar feels and how much he has to be on his guard throughout the speech.*

• *Find a way for Edgar to exit the scene.*

WHERE ELSE TO LOOK ☞    *Caliban (The Tempest, p. 18) and Trinculo (The Tempest, p. 20) are both exposed to the elements and seeking refuge.*

## *Edgar*

**❝** I heard myself proclaim'd,*
And by the happy hollow of a tree
Escap'd the hunt. No port is free, no place
That guard and most unusual vigilance
Does not attend my taking.* Whiles I may scape,
I will preserve myself, and am bethought*
To take the basest and most poorest shape
That ever penury, in contempt of man,
Brought near to beast.* My face I'll grime with filth,
Blanket my loins, elf* all my hair in knots,
And with presented nakedness outface
The winds and persecutions of the sky.
The country gives me proof and precedent
Of Bedlam beggars,* who with roaring voices,
Strike in their numb'd and mortifièd* arms
Pins, wooden pricks, nails, sprigs of rosemary;
And with this horrible object, from low farms,
Poor pelting* villages, sheep-cotes, and mills,
Sometime with lunatic bans, sometime with prayers,
Enforce their charity. 'Poor Turlygod! Poor Tom!'
That's something yet; Edgar I nothing am. **❞**

(*Act 2, scene 2, lines 164–84*)

GLOSSARY

*proclaim'd* – declared an outlaw, shouted after
*no place / That guard and most unusual vigilance / Does not attend my
taking* – there is no place that is not guarded with extra vigilance to
look out for me
*am bethought* – I think
*penury, in contempt of man, / Brought near to beast* – poverty scorned
mankind by transforming him into a mere animal
*elf* – tangle
*Bedlam beggars* – beggars from the Bethlehem Hospital for the insane
*mortifièd* – deadened
*pelting* – worthless

# Othello

WHO ☞ *Iago, a villainous 'ensign' or aide to Othello, a noble Moor in the service of the Venetian State.*

WHERE ☞ *A council-chamber in Venice, perhaps contemporaneous with Shakespeare.*

WHO ELSE IS THERE ☞ *Iago is alone.*

WHAT IS HAPPENING ☞ *Overwhelmed with his hatred of his superior Othello, Iago comes up with a plan during the speech to convince Othello that Cassio (another officer promoted over the head of Iago) is having an affair with his wife.*

WHAT TO THINK ABOUT ☞

* *Iago does not use Othello's name at first but just calls him 'the Moor', a racial description, perhaps as a term of abuse.*

* *His first line is just four strong single-syllable words. The pattern follows through the speech: 'He holds me well', 'Let me see now', 'How? How? Let's see'.*

* *What is it that he so hates about Othello? Decide whether he really believes Othello to have been ''twixt my sheets' with his wife, or whether he is just using this as a pretext for his hatred.*

* *Cassio is his rival and has been promoted over Iago.*

* *He takes time to come up with a plan: 'How? How? Let's see.' Allow time for the plan to come into being.*

* *After so many short words Iago can relish 'engender'd'.*

* *Decide how much of his speech Iago is sharing with the audience.*

WHERE ELSE TO LOOK ☞ *Also contemplating revenge are Alcibiades (Timon of Athens, p. 96) and Hamlet (Hamlet, p. 108). Unashamed of their villainy are Aaron (Titus Andronicus, p. 92) and Edmund (King Lear, p. 110).*

## *Iago*

**"** I hate the Moor,
And it is thought abroad, that 'twixt my sheets
He has done my office. I know not if 't be true,
But I, for mere suspicion in that kind,
Will do as if for surety. He holds me well:*
The better shall my purpose work on him.
Cassio's a proper* man. Let me see now:
To get his place and to plume up my will*
In double knavery.* How? How? Let's see.
After some time to abuse Othello's ears
That he is too familiar with his wife.
He hath a person and a smooth dispose*
To be suspected, fram'd to make women false;
The Moor is of a free and open nature
That thinks men honest that but seem to be so,
And will as tenderly be led by th' nose
As asses are.
I have't! It is engender'd. Hell and night
Must bring this monstrous birth to the world's light. **"**

*(Act 1, scene 3, lines 392–410)*

GLOSSARY

*He holds me well* – he respects me
*proper* – good-looking
*plume up my will* – put a feather in my cap
*double knavery* – he will both take Cassio's place and cause trouble for
    Othello
*smooth dispose* – genial disposition

# Othello

WHO ☞ *Othello, a noble Moor in the service of the Venetian State.*

WHERE ☞ *In the bedroom of his wife Desdemona, in the garrison on Cyprus, perhaps contemporaneous with Shakespeare.*

WHO ELSE IS THERE ☞ *His wife Desdemona is asleep in the room.*

WHAT IS HAPPENING ☞ *Thinking that she has been unfaithful to him, Othello comes to kill his wife Desdemona. Only the light of a candle illuminates the room.*

WHAT TO THINK ABOUT ☞

- *The cause of Othello's action is Desdemona's supposed unfaithfulness.*

- *Although Othello is alone with the sleeping Desdemona, both the lighted candle and his own soul are spoken to.*

- *It is night and Othello sees by candle light. Create the sense of time and atmosphere that implies.*

- *Picture how white and beautiful Desdemona looks and how careful Othello must be not to wake her.*

- *Decide where he fluctuates in his resolve to kill her.*

- *He kisses her and then kisses her again, moments so tender that he feels and smells her breath.*

WHERE ELSE TO LOOK ☞ *Posthumus (Cymbeline, p. 120) and Antony (Antony and Cleopatra, p. 118) are also torn apart by what they think to be the unfaithfulness of their wives.*

## *Othello*

**❝** It is the cause, it is the cause, my soul.
Let me not name it to you, you chaste stars.
It is the cause. Yet I'll not shed her blood,
Nor scar that whiter skin of hers than snow
And smooth as monumental alabaster.
Yet she must die, else she'll betray more men.
Put out the light – and then put out the light.
If I quench thee, thou flaming minister,*
I can again thy former light restore,
Should I repent me; but once put out thy light,
Thou cunning'st pattern of excelling nature,
I know not where is that Promethean heat*
That can thy light relume. When I have pluck'd the rose,
I cannot give it vital growth again;
It must needs wither. I'll smell it on the tree.

*Kissing her.*

O balmy breath, that dost almost persuade
Justice to break her sword! One more, one more!
Be thus when thou art dead, and I will kill thee
And love thee after. One more, and that's the last:
So sweet was ne'er so fatal. I must weep,
But they are cruel tears. This sorrow's heavenly;
It strikes where it doth love. She wakes. **❞**

(*Act 5, scene 2, lines 1–22*)

GLOSSARY

*flaming minister* – the candle by Desdemona's bed
*Promethean heat* – in Greek mythology Prometheus was the mortal who
    stole fire from the gods

# Antony and Cleopatra

WHO ☞ *Mark Antony.*

WHERE ☞ *Between the rival camps of the Roman and Egyptian armies at the battle of Alexandria, 31 July, 30 BC.*

WHO ELSE IS THERE ☞ *Scarus, a friend of Antony.*

WHAT IS HAPPENING ☞ *Antony was once one of the triumvirate ruling the Roman Empire, but became lover of Cleopatra, Queen of Egypt. Cleopatra and the Egyptians are at war against Caesar and the Romans. The battle is lost and Antony believes himself to have been betrayed by Cleopatra, 'this foul Egyptian'.*

WHAT TO THINK ABOUT ☞

- *The speech starts with a single three syllable sentence, simple and bleak.*

- *Antony is dealing with his defeat in battle and with the betrayal of his lover.*

- *Decide how unexpected Cleopatra's betrayal is.*

- *The speech is at once personal, political and military. Antony's thoughts and emotions constantly move between these related points. He thinks of Cleopatra, then of Caesar, then of his soldiers, then of himself and then again of Cleopatra.*

- *There is a simplicity about the short sentences 'All is lost' and later 'Betray'd I am', which anchor the rest of the speech.*

WHERE ELSE TO LOOK ☞ *Other men believing themselves to have been deceived by their wives are Othello (Othello, p. 116) and Posthumus (Cymbeline, p. 120).*

## *Mark Antony*

66 All is lost.
This foul Egyptian hath betrayèd me.
My fleet hath yielded to the foe, and yonder
They cast their caps up, and carouse together
Like friends long lost. Triple-turn'd* whore, 'tis thou
Hast sold me to this novice,* and my heart
Makes only wars on thee. Bid them all fly.
For when I am reveng'd upon my charm,
I have done all. Bid them all fly, begone!
O sun, thy uprise shall I see no more.
Fortune and Antony part here, even here
Do we shake hands. All come to this? The hearts
That spaniel'd me at heels,* to whom I gave
Their wishes, do discandy,* melt their sweets
On blossoming Caesar. And this pine is bark'd,*
That overtopp'd them all. Betray'd I am.
O this false soul of Egypt! This grave charm,
Whose eye beck'd forth* my wars, and call'd them home,
Whose bosom was my crownet,* my chief end,
Like a right gypsy, hath at fast and loose
Beguil'd me to the very heart of loss. 99

(*Act 4, scene 13, lines 9–29*)

GLOSSARY

*triple-turn'd* – double-crossing
*novice* – i.e. the young Octavius Caesar
*spaniel'd me at heels* – followed me like puppies
*discandy* – dissolve (change sides and leave Antony for Caesar)
*this pine is bark'd* – this tree (i.e. Antony) is stripped of its bark and so
    destroyed
*beck'd forth* – summoned, called into being
*crownet* – coronet

# Cymbeline

WHO ☞ *Posthumus, banished husband of Imogen, daughter of Cymbeline, the King of England.*

WHERE ☞ *A room in the house of Philario, Posthumus's host in Rome, c. 40 AD.*

WHO ELSE IS THERE ☞ *Posthumus is alone.*

WHAT IS HAPPENING ☞ *Posthumus has been banished for secretly marrying Imogen, daughter of the King of England. He has gone to Rome where he has boasted of his wife's virtue. The villain Iachimo deceives Posthumus into believing that he has slept with Imogen.*

WHAT TO THINK ABOUT ☞

- *Posthumus's speech is full of loathing.*
- *His feelings turn in on himself rather than being directed out at his wife.*
- *He blames all women rather than just Imogen.*
- *Posthumus appears to be on the verge of madness during the speech.*
- *The word 'hers' is repeated with possibly increasing venom.*
- *In his frustration all Posthumus can think of for revenge is to 'write against them, / Detest them, curse them'.*

WHERE ELSE TO LOOK ☞ *Othello (Othello, p. 116) and Antony (Antony and Cleopatra, p. 118) are also torn apart by what they think to be the unfaithfulness of their wives.*

### Posthumus

❝ Is there no way for men to be, but women
Must be half-workers?* We are all bastards,
And that most venerable man, which I
Did call my father, was I know not where
When I was stamp'd. Some coiner* with his tools
Made me a counterfeit. Yet my mother seem'd

The Dian* of that time. So doth my wife
The nonpareil* of this. Oh, vengeance, vengeance!
Me of my lawful pleasure she restrain'd,
And pray'd me oft forbearance; did it with
A pudency* so rosy, the sweet view on't
Might well have warm'd old Saturn; that I thought her
As chaste as unsunn'd snow. Oh, all the devils!
This yellow Iachimo in an hour, was't not?
Or less; at first? Perchance he spoke not, but
Like a full-acorn'd boar,* a German one,
Cried 'Oh!' and mounted; found no opposition
But what he look'd for should oppose, and she
Should from encounter guard. Could I find out
The woman's part in me – for there's no motion
That tends to vice in man but I affirm
It is the woman's part. Be it lying, note it,
The woman's; flattering, hers; deceiving, hers;
Lust and rank thoughts, hers, hers; revenges, hers;
Ambitions, covetings, change of prides, disdain,
Nice* longing, slanders, mutability,
All faults that man may name, nay, that hell knows,
Why, hers, in part or all; but rather all;
For even to vice
They are not constant, but are changing still,
One vice but of a minute old, for one
Not half so old as that. I'll write against them,
Detest them, curse them. Yet 'tis greater skill
In a true hate to pray they have their will.
The very devils cannot plague them better. **99**

(*Act 2, scene 5, whole scene*)

GLOSSARY

*half-workers* – collaborators          *coiner* – forger
*Dian* – Diana, the goddess of chastity
*nonpareil* – person without equal (pronounced '*non-pe-rail*')
*pudency* – modesty
*full-acorn'd boar* – a boar fattened with acorns (an image of a gross
    animal, the more gross for being German)
*nice* – lecherous